COOKING
for KIDS

CONTENTS

BREAKFAST

whip 'em up wacky waffles

1½ cups biscuit baking mix

1 cup buttermilk

1 large egg

1 tablespoon vegetable oil

½ cup "M&M's"® Semi-Sweet Chocolate Mini Baking Bits

Powdered sugar and maple syrup

Preheat Belgian waffle iron. In large bowl combine baking mix, buttermilk, egg and oil until well mixed. Spoon about ½ cup batter into hot waffle iron. Sprinkle with about 2 tablespoons "M&M's"® Semi-Sweet Chocolate Mini Baking Bits; top with about ½ cup batter. Close lid and bake until steaming stops, 1 to 2 minutes.* Sprinkle with powdered sugar and serve immediately with maple syrup and additional "M&M's"® Semi-Sweet Chocolate Mini Baking Bits.   *makes 4 Belgian waffles*

Check the manufacturer's directions for recommended amount of batter and baking time.

chocolate waffles: Substitute 1¼ cups biscuit baking mix, ¼ cup unsweetened cocoa powder and ½ cup sugar for 1½ cups biscuit baking mix. Prepare and cook as directed above.

tip: These waffles make a great dessert too! Serve them with a scoop of ice cream, chocolate sauce and a sprinkle of "M&M's"® Chocolate Mini Baking Bits.

banana blueberry muffins

2 ripe, medium DOLE® Bananas
6 tablespoons margarine
6 tablespoons brown sugar
1 egg
1½ cups all-purpose flour
½ teaspoon baking powder
½ teaspoon baking soda
½ teaspoon salt
½ teaspoon grated lemon peel
1 cup frozen blueberries, rinsed, drained

• Purée bananas in blender (1 cup).

• Beat margarine and sugar in large bowl until light and fluffy. Mix in bananas and egg.

• Combine flour, baking powder, baking soda, salt and lemon peel in medium bowl. Blend into margarine mixture just until moistened. Fold in blueberries.

• Line 6 large muffin cups with paper liners; spray lightly with vegetable cooking spray. Spoon batter evenly into cups.

• Bake at 375°F 20 to 25 minutes.

makes 6 muffins

prep time: 20 minutes
bake time: 25 minutes

super cinnamon bun

CINNAMON BUN

1 (16 ounce) package hot roll mix

1 cup QUAKER® Oats (quick or old fashioned, uncooked)

¾ cup raisins

½ cup sugar, divided

2½ teaspoons ground cinnamon, divided

1 cup hot water (120°F to 130°F)

1 egg, lightly beaten

5 tablespoons margarine or butter, melted, divided

GLAZE

¾ cup powdered sugar

3 to 4 teaspoons milk

½ teaspoon vanilla

Lightly grease large cookie sheet. In large bowl, combine hot roll mix, yeast packet, oats, raisins, ¼ cup sugar and 1½ teaspoons cinnamon. Stir in hot water, egg and 3 tablespoons melted margarine. Mix until dough pulls away from sides of bowl. Knead on lightly floured surface 5 minutes or until smooth and elastic. Divide into 4 equal pieces; roll each piece into 12-inch rope on lightly floured surface. In center of prepared cookie sheet, form a coil with one rope. Attach a second rope to the coiled rope by pressing the rope ends together firmly; continue coiling around the first rope. Repeat with the third and fourth ropes to form one large bun.

Combine remaining ¼ cup sugar, 1 teaspoon cinnamon and 2 tablespoons melted margarine. Brush evenly over top and sides of bun. Cover loosely with plastic wrap; let rise in warm place 30 minutes or until about double in size.

Heat oven to 375°F. Bake 30 to 35 minutes or until golden brown. Carefully remove to wire rack; cool slightly. For glaze, combine all ingredients; mix until smooth. Drizzle over bun. Serve warm or at room temperature.

makes 16 servings

note: If the hot roll mix is not available, combine 3 cups all-purpose flour, 1 cup oats, ¾ cup raisins, two ¼-ounce packages quick-rising yeast, ⅓ cup granulated sugar, 1½ teaspoons salt and 1½ teaspoons cinnamon. Continue as recipe directs.

banana smoothies & pops

1 (14-ounce) can
  EAGLE® BRAND
  Sweetened
  Condensed Milk
  (NOT evaporated
  milk)
1 (8-ounce) container
  vanilla yogurt
2 ripe bananas
½ cup orange juice

Process Eagle Brand and remaining ingredients in blender until smooth, stopping to scrape down sides. Serve immediately.   *makes 4 cups*

banana smoothie pops: Spoon banana mixture into 8 (5-ounce) paper cups. Freeze 30 minutes. Insert wooden craft sticks into center of each cup; freeze until firm.

fruit smoothies: Substitute 1 cup of your favorite fruit and ½ cup any fruit juice for banana and orange juice.

prep time: 5 minutes

buttermilk pancakes

2 cups all-purpose flour
1 tablespoon sugar
1½ teaspoons baking
  powder
½ teaspoon baking soda
½ teaspoon salt
1 egg, beaten
1½ cups buttermilk
¼ cup vegetable oil

1. Sift flour, sugar, baking powder, baking soda and salt into large bowl.

2. Combine egg, buttermilk and oil in medium bowl. Stir liquid ingredients into dry ingredients until moistened.

3. Preheat griddle or large skillet over medium heat; grease lightly. Pour about ½ cup batter onto hot griddle for each pancake. Cook until tops of pancakes are bubbly and appear dry; turn and cook until browned, about 2 minutes.   *makes about 12 (5-inch) pancakes*

silver dollar pancakes: Use 1 tablespoon batter for each pancake. Cook as directed above.

buttermilk substitution: If you don't have buttermilk on hand, try this easy substitution. Place 1 tablespoon vinegar in measuring cup. Add milk to measure 1½ cups. Stir well; let stand 5 minutes.

BREAKFAST

chocolate quickie stickies

8 tablespoons (1 stick)
   butter or margarine,
   divided

¾ cup packed light
   brown sugar

4 tablespoons
   HERSHEY'S Cocoa,
   divided

5 teaspoons water

1 teaspoon vanilla
   extract

½ cup coarsely chopped
   nuts (optional)

2 cans (8 ounces each)
   refrigerated quick
   crescent dinner rolls

2 tablespoons
   granulated sugar

1. Heat oven to 350°F.

2. Melt 6 tablespoons butter in small saucepan over low heat; add brown sugar, 3 tablespoons cocoa and water. Cook over medium heat, stirring constantly, just until mixture comes to boil. Remove from heat; stir in vanilla. Spoon about 1 teaspoon chocolate mixture into each of 48 small muffin cups (1¾ inches in diameter). Sprinkle ½ teaspoon nuts, if desired, into each cup; set aside.

3. Unroll dough; separate into 8 rectangles; firmly press perforations to seal. Melt remaining 2 tablespoons butter; brush over rectangles. Stir together granulated sugar and remaining 1 tablespoon cocoa; sprinkle over rectangles. Starting at longer side, roll up each rectangle; pinch seams to seal. Cut each roll into 6 equal pieces. Press gently into prepared pans, cut-side down.

4. Bake 11 to 13 minutes or until light brown. Remove from oven; let cool 30 seconds. Invert onto cookie sheet. Let stand 1 minute; remove pans. Serve warm or cool completely.   *makes 4 dozen small rolls*

note: Rolls can be baked in two 8-inch round baking pans. Heat oven to 350°F. Cook chocolate mixture as directed; spread half of mixture in each pan. Prepare rolls as directed; place 24 pieces, cut-side down, in each pan. Bake 20 to 22 minutes. Cool and remove pans as directed above.

8

french toast sticks

1 cup EGG BEATERS®
Healthy Real Egg
Product

⅓ cup skim milk

1 teaspoon ground
cinnamon

1 teaspoon vanilla
extract

2 tablespoons
FLEISCHMANN'S®
Original Margarine,
divided

16 (4×1×1-inch) sticks
day-old white bread

Powdered sugar,
optional

Maple-flavored syrup,
optional

In shallow bowl, combine Egg Beaters®, milk, cinnamon and vanilla.

In large nonstick griddle or skillet, over medium-high heat, melt 2 teaspoons margarine. Dip bread sticks in egg mixture to coat; transfer to griddle. Cook sticks on each side until golden, adding remaining margarine as needed. Dust lightly with powdered sugar and serve with syrup, if desired.

makes 4 servings

prep time: 15 minutes
cook time: 18 minutes

fruit 'n juice breakfast shake

1 extra-ripe, medium
DOLE® Banana

¾ cup DOLE® Pineapple
Juice

½ cup low fat vanilla
yogurt

½ cup blueberries

Combine all ingredients in blender. Whir until smooth.

makes 2 servings

breakfast pizza

1 can (10 ounces) refrigerated biscuit dough

½ pound bacon slices

2 tablespoons butter or margarine

2 tablespoons all-purpose flour

¼ teaspoon salt

⅛ teaspoon black pepper

1½ cups milk

½ cup (2 ounces) shredded sharp Cheddar cheese

¼ cup sliced green onion

¼ cup chopped red bell pepper

Preheat oven to 350°F. Spray 13×9-inch baking dish with nonstick cooking spray.

Separate biscuit dough and arrange in rectangle on lightly floured surface. Roll into 14×10-inch rectangle. Place in prepared dish; pat edges up sides of dish. Bake 15 minutes. Remove from oven and set aside.

Meanwhile, place bacon in single layer in large skillet; cook over medium heat until crisp. Remove from skillet; drain on paper towels. Crumble and set aside.

Melt butter in medium saucepan over medium heat. Stir in flour, salt and black pepper until smooth. Gradually stir in milk; cook and stir until thickened. Stir in cheese until melted. Spread sauce evenly over baked crust. Arrange bacon, green onions and bell pepper over sauce.

Bake, uncovered, 20 minutes or until crust is golden brown.

makes 6 servings

Bacon can be cooked in the oven instead of in a skillet. Simply place bacon strips in a single layer on a baking sheet with sides and bake in a preheated 400°F oven for 10 to 15 minutes. Drain on paper towels before using.

bunny pancakes with strawberry butter

Strawberry Butter
(recipe follows)

2 cups buttermilk
baking mix

1 cup milk

2 eggs

½ cup plain yogurt

Assorted candies

1. Prepare Strawberry Butter; set aside. Preheat electric skillet or griddle to 375°F.

2. Combine baking mix, milk, eggs and yogurt in medium bowl; mix well. Spoon scant ½ cup batter into skillet. With back of spoon, gently spread batter into 4-inch circle. Spoon about 2 tablespoons batter onto top edge of circle for head. Using back of spoon, spread batter from head to form bunny ears as shown in photo.

3. Cook until bubbles on surface begin to pop and top of pancake appears dry; turn pancake over. Cook until done, 1 to 2 minutes. Decorate with candies as shown in photo.

4. Repeat with remaining batter. Serve warm with Strawberry Butter.

makes about 12 pancakes

strawberry butter: Place 1 package (3 ounces) softened cream cheese and ½ cup softened butter in food processor or blender; process until smooth. Add ⅓ cup powdered sugar; process until blended. Add 1½ cups fresh or thawed frozen strawberries; process until finely chopped.

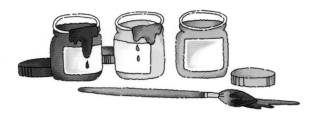

bunny pancakes with strawberry butter

peanut butter & jelly french toast

¼ cup strawberry or favorite flavor jam or preserves

6 slices whole wheat bread, divided

¼ cup peanut butter

2 eggs

¼ cup milk

2 tablespoons butter

1½ tablespoons orange juice

1½ tablespoons honey

1 large ripe banana, sliced

2 tablespoons chopped peanuts

1. Spread jam evenly over 3 slices bread. Spread peanut butter evenly over remaining 3 slices bread. Press slices together to form 3 sandwiches; cut each sandwich diagonally in half.

2. Combine eggs and milk in shallow bowl. Coat each sandwich with egg mixture.

3. Melt butter on large nonstick griddle or in skillet over medium-high heat; cook sandwiches 2 minutes on each side or until golden. Set aside and keep warm.

4. Blend orange juice and honey in small bowl; stir in banana and peanuts. Arrange sandwiches on platter; top with banana mixture.

makes 6 servings

prep time: 25 minutes
cook time: 10 minutes

Bananas will ripen if they are kept uncovered at room temperature. To speed up the ripening process, place them in a perforated brown paper bag with a ripe apple.

14

fruit muffins

MUFFINS

⅔ cup milk

1 tablespoon oil

1 egg

2 cups packaged baking mix

2 tablespoons sugar

¼ cup SMUCKER'S® Preserves (any flavor)

GLAZE

⅔ cup powdered sugar

3 to 4 teaspoons milk

Grease bottom only of 12 medium muffin cups or line with paper baking cups. Combine milk, oil and egg; blend until well mixed. Add baking mix and sugar; stir just until moistened. Fill greased muffin cups ⅔ full. Drop 1 level teaspoon of preserves onto center of batter in each cup.

Bake at 400°F for 13 to 18 minutes or until golden brown. Cool slightly and remove from pan.

Stir together glaze ingredients until smooth, adding enough milk for desired glaze consistency. Drizzle over cooled muffins.

makes 12 muffins

ham & swiss cheese biscuits

2 cups all-purpose flour

2 teaspoons baking powder

½ teaspoon baking soda

½ cup butter, chilled and cut into pieces

½ cup (2 ounces) shredded Swiss cheese

2 ounces ham, minced

About ⅔ cup buttermilk

1. Preheat oven to 450°F. Grease baking sheet.

2. Sift flour, baking powder and baking soda into medium bowl. Using pastry blender or 2 knives, cut in butter until mixture resembles coarse crumbs. Stir in cheese, ham and enough buttermilk to make soft dough.

3. Turn out dough onto lightly floured surface; knead lightly. Roll out dough ½ inch thick. Cut biscuit rounds with 2-inch cutter. Place on greased baking sheet.

4. Bake about 10 minutes or until browned.

makes about 18 biscuits

apple raisin pancakes

- **2 cups all-purpose flour**
- **2 tablespoons sugar**
- **1 tablespoon baking powder**
- **2 teaspoons ground cinnamon**
- **1¾ cups fat-free (skim) milk**
- **⅔ cup EGG BEATERS® Healthy Real Egg Product**
- **5 tablespoons FLEISCHMANN'S® Original Margarine, melted, divided**
- **¾ cup chopped apple**
- **¾ cup seedless raisins**

In large bowl, combine flour, sugar, baking powder and cinnamon. In medium bowl, combine milk, Egg Beaters® and 4 tablespoons margarine; stir into dry ingredients just until blended. Stir in apple and raisins.

Brush large nonstick griddle or skillet with some of remaining margarine; heat over medium-high heat. Using ¼ cup batter for each pancake, pour batter onto griddle. Cook until bubbly; turn and cook until lightly browned. Repeat with remaining batter using remaining margarine as needed to make 16 pancakes.

makes 16 (4-inch) pancakes

prep time: 10 minutes
cook time: 15 minutes

chocolate chip waffles

1 package DUNCAN HINES® Chocolate Chip Muffin Mix

¾ cup all-purpose flour

1 teaspoon baking powder

1¾ cups milk

2 eggs

5 tablespoons butter or margarine, melted

Confectioners' sugar (optional)

Preheat and lightly grease waffle iron according to manufacturer's directions.

Combine muffin mix, flour and baking powder in large bowl. Add milk, eggs and melted butter. Stir until moistened, about 50 strokes. Pour batter onto center grids of preheated waffle iron. Bake according to manufacturer's directions until golden brown. Remove baked waffle carefully with fork. Repeat with remaining batter. Dust lightly with sugar, if desired. Top with fresh fruit, syrup, grated chocolate or whipped cream, if desired. *makes 10 to 12 waffles*

banana chocolate chip muffins

2 ripe, medium DOLE® Bananas

2 eggs

1 cup packed brown sugar

½ cup margarine, melted

1 teaspoon vanilla extract

2¼ cups all-purpose flour

2 teaspoons baking powder

½ teaspoon ground cinnamon

½ teaspoon salt

1 cup chocolate chips

½ cup chopped walnuts

• Purée bananas in blender (1 cup). Beat bananas, eggs, sugar, margarine and vanilla in medium bowl until well blended.

• Combine flour, baking powder, cinnamon and salt in large bowl. Stir in chocolate chips and nuts. Make well in center of dry ingredients. Add banana mixture. Stir just until blended. Spoon into well greased 2½-inch muffin pan cups.

• Bake at 350°F, 25 to 30 minutes or until toothpick inserted in center comes out clean. Cool slightly, remove from pan and place on wire rack. *makes 12 muffins*

prep time: 20 minutes
bake time: 30 minutes

apple & raisin oven pancake

1 large baking apple, cored and thinly sliced

⅓ cup golden raisins

2 tablespoons packed brown sugar

½ teaspoon ground cinnamon

4 eggs

⅔ cup milk

⅔ cup all-purpose flour

2 tablespoons butter or margarine, melted

Powdered sugar (optional)

Preheat oven to 350°F. Spray 9-inch pie plate with nonstick cooking spray.

Combine apple, raisins, brown sugar and cinnamon in medium bowl. Transfer to prepared pie plate.

Bake, uncovered, 10 to 15 minutes or until apple begins to soften. Remove from oven. *Increase oven temperature to 450°F.*

Meanwhile, whisk eggs, milk, flour and butter in medium bowl until blended. Pour batter over apple mixture.

Bake 15 minutes or until pancake is golden brown. Invert onto serving dish. Sprinkle with powdered sugar, if desired.   *makes 6 servings*

maple apple oatmeal

2 cups apple juice

1½ cups water

⅓ cup AUNT JEMIMA® Syrup

½ teaspoon ground cinnamon

¼ teaspoon salt (optional)

2 cups QUAKER® Oats (quick or old fashioned, uncooked)

1 cup chopped fresh unpeeled apple (about 1 medium)

In 3-quart saucepan, bring juice, water, syrup, cinnamon and salt to a boil. Stir in oats and apple. Return to a boil; reduce heat to medium-low. Cook about 1 minute for quick oats (or 5 minutes for old fashioned oats) or until most of liquid is absorbed, stirring occasionally. Let stand until of desired consistency.   *makes 4 servings*

orange cinnamon swirl bread

BREAD

1 package DUNCAN HINES® Cinnamon Swirl Muffin Mix

1 egg

⅔ cup orange juice

1 tablespoon grated orange peel

ORANGE GLAZE

½ cup confectioners' sugar

2 to 3 teaspoons orange juice

1 teaspoon grated orange peel

Quartered orange slices, for garnish (optional)

1. Preheat oven to 350°F. Grease and flour 8½×4½×2½-inch loaf pan.

2. For bread, combine muffin mix and contents of topping packet from mix in large bowl. Break up any lumps. Add egg, ⅔ cup orange juice and 1 tablespoon orange peel. Stir until moistened, about 50 strokes. Knead swirl packet from mix for 10 seconds before opening. Squeeze contents on top of batter. Swirl into batter with knife or spatula, folding from bottom of bowl to get an even swirl. *Do not completely mix in.* Pour into pan. Bake at 350°F 55 to 60 minutes or until toothpick inserted in center comes out clean. Cool in pan 10 minutes. Loosen loaf from pan. Invert onto cooling rack. Turn right side up. Cool completely.

3. For orange glaze, place confectioners' sugar in small bowl. Add orange juice, 1 teaspoon at a time, stirring until smooth and desired consistency. Stir in 1 teaspoon orange peel. Drizzle over loaf. Garnish with orange slices, if desired.

makes 1 loaf (12 slices)

tip: If glaze becomes too thin, add more confectioners' sugar. If glaze is too thick, add more orange juice.

creamy cinnamon rolls

2 (1-pound) loaves frozen bread dough, thawed

⅔ cup (one-half 14-ounce can) EAGLE® BRAND Sweetened Condensed Milk (NOT evaporated milk), divided*

1 cup chopped pecans

2 teaspoons ground cinnamon

1 cup sifted powdered sugar

½ teaspoon vanilla extract

Additional chopped pecans (optional)

*Use remaining Eagle Brand as a dip for fruit. Pour into storage container and store tightly covered in refrigerator for up to 1 week.

1. On lightly floured surface roll each of bread dough loaves to 12×9-inch rectangle. Spread ⅓ cup Eagle Brand over dough rectangles. Sprinkle with 1 cup pecans and cinnamon. Roll up jelly-roll style starting from a short side. Cut each into 6 slices.

2. Generously grease 13×9-inch baking pan. Place rolls cut sides down in pan. Cover loosely with greased waxed paper and then with plastic wrap. Chill overnight. Cover and chill remaining Eagle Brand.

3. To bake, let pan of rolls stand at room temperature for 30 minutes. Preheat oven to 350°F. Bake 30 to 35 minutes or until golden brown. Cool in pan 5 minutes; loosen edges and remove rolls from pan.

4. Meanwhile for frosting, in small bowl, combine powdered sugar, remaining ⅓ cup Eagle Brand and vanilla. Drizzle frosting on warm rolls. Sprinkle with additional chopped pecans.   *makes 12 rolls*

prep time: 20 minutes
bake time: 30 to 35 minutes
chill time: overnight
cool time: 5 minutes

tooty fruitys

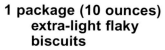

1 package (10 ounces)
extra-light flaky
biscuits
10 (1½-inch) fruit pieces
1 egg white
1 teaspoon water
Powdered sugar
(optional)

1. Preheat oven to 425°F. Spray baking sheets with nonstick cooking spray; set aside.

2. Separate biscuits. Place on lightly floured surface. Roll with lightly floured rolling pin or flatten dough with fingers to form 3½-inch circles. Place 1 fruit piece in center of each circle. Bring 3 edges of dough up over fruit; pinch edges together to seal. Place on prepared baking sheet.

3. Beat egg white with water in small bowl; brush over dough.

4. Bake until golden brown, 10 to 15 minutes. Remove to wire rack to cool. Serve warm or at room temperature. Sprinkle with powdered sugar just before serving. *makes 10 servings*

sweet tooty fruitys: Prepare dough circles as directed. Gently press both sides of dough circles into granulated or cinnamon-sugar to coat completely. Top with fruit and continue as directed, except do not brush with egg white mixture or sprinkle with powdered sugar.

cheesy tooty fruitys: Prepare dough circles as directed. Top each circle with ½ teaspoon softened reduced-fat cream cheese in addition to the fruit. Continue as directed.

sugar and cinnamon apple muffins

MUFFINS

1 egg

⅔ cup apple juice or milk

½ cup oil

1 teaspoon vanilla

2 cups all-purpose flour

¼ cup DOMINO® Granulated Sugar

¼ cup firmly packed DOMINO® Light Brown Sugar

1 tablespoon baking powder

½ teaspoon salt

1½ cups cored and chopped apple

½ cup chopped nuts

TOPPING

2 tablespoons DOMINO® Granulated Sugar

1 teaspoon cinnamon

Heat oven to 400°F. Grease bottoms of 12 medium muffin cups or line with paper baking cups.

Beat egg with juice, oil and vanilla in medium bowl. Stir in flour, sugars, baking powder and salt just until flour is moistened (batter will be lumpy). Stir in apple and nuts. Fill muffin cups.

Combine topping ingredients in small bowl; sprinkle over batter in muffin cups.

Bake at 400°F. for 20 to 22 minutes or until golden brown. Immediately remove from pan to cooling rack.

makes 12 muffins

prep time: 20 minutes
bake time: 22 minutes

Don't stir muffin batter too vigorously or you'll end up with tough muffins. Just stir until all the dry ingredients are moistened; any lumps will disappear during baking.

cinnamon fruit crunch

1 cup low-fat granola cereal

¼ cup toasted sliced almonds

1 tablespoon margarine

2 tablespoons plus 1 teaspoon packed brown sugar, divided

2¼ teaspoons ground cinnamon, divided

½ cup vanilla yogurt

⅛ teaspoon ground nutmeg

2 cans (16 ounces each) mixed fruit chunks in juice, drained

Combine granola and almonds in small bowl. Melt margarine in small saucepan. Blend in 2 tablespoons brown sugar and 2 teaspoons cinnamon; simmer until sugar dissolves, about 2 minutes. Toss with granola and almonds; cool. Combine yogurt, remaining 1 teaspoon brown sugar, ¼ teaspoon cinnamon and nutmeg in small bowl. To serve, spoon approximately ½ cup chunky mixed fruit onto each serving plate. Top with yogurt mixture and sprinkle with granola mixture.

makes 6 servings

orange smoothies

1 cup fat-free vanilla ice cream or fat-free vanilla frozen yogurt

¾ cup low-fat (1%) milk

¼ cup frozen orange juice concentrate

1. Combine ice cream, milk and orange juice concentrate in food processor or blender; process until smooth.

2. Pour mixture into 2 glasses; garnish as desired. Serve immediately.

makes 2 servings

chocolate quicky sticky bread

2 loaves (16 ounces each) frozen bread dough

¾ cup granulated sugar

1 tablespoon HERSHEY'S Cocoa

1 teaspoon ground cinnamon

½ cup (1 stick) butter or margarine, melted and divided

½ cup packed light brown sugar

¼ cup water

HERSHEY'S MINI KISSES™ Semi-Sweet or Milk Chocolate Baking Pieces

1. Thaw loaves as directed on package; let rise until doubled.

2. Stir together granulated sugar, cocoa and cinnamon. In small microwave-safe bowl, stir together ¼ cup butter, brown sugar and water. Microwave at HIGH (100%) 30 to 60 seconds or until smooth when stirred. Pour mixture into 12-cup fluted tube pan.

3. Heat oven to 350°F. Pinch off pieces of bread dough; form into balls, 1½ inches in diameter, placing 3 Mini Kisses™ inside each ball. Dip each ball in remaining ¼ cup butter; roll in cocoa-sugar mixture. Place balls in prepared pan.

4. Bake 45 to 50 minutes or until golden brown. Cool 20 minutes in pan; invert onto serving plate. Cool until lukewarm.

makes 12 servings

peanut butter mini muffins

⅓ cup creamy peanut butter

¼ cup (½ stick) butter, softened

¼ cup granulated sugar

¼ cup firmly packed light brown sugar

1 large egg

¾ cup buttermilk

3 tablespoons vegetable oil

¾ teaspoon vanilla extract

1½ cups all-purpose flour

¾ teaspoon baking powder

½ teaspoon baking soda

½ teaspoon salt

1¼ cups "M&M's"® Milk Chocolate Mini Baking Bits, divided

Chocolate Glaze (recipe follows)

Preheat oven to 350°F. Lightly grease 36 (1¾-inch) mini muffin cups or line with paper or foil liners; set aside. In large bowl cream peanut butter, butter and sugars until light and fluffy; beat in egg. Beat in buttermilk, oil and vanilla. In medium bowl combine flour, baking powder, baking soda and salt; gradually blend into creamed mixture. Divide batter evenly among prepared muffin cups. Sprinkle batter evenly with ¾ cup "M&M's"® Milk Chocolate Mini Baking Bits. Bake 15 to 17 minutes or until toothpick inserted in centers comes out clean. Cool completely on wire racks. Prepare Chocolate Glaze. Place glaze in resealable plastic sandwich bag; seal bag. Cut tiny piece off one corner of bag (not more than ⅛ inch). Drizzle glaze over muffins. Decorate with remaining ½ cup "M&M's"® Milk Chocolate Mini Baking Bits. Store in tightly covered container. *makes 3 dozen mini muffins*

chocolate glaze: In top of double boiler over hot water, melt 2 (1-ounce) squares semi-sweet chocolate and 1 tablespoon butter. Stir until smooth; let cool slightly.

30

cereal trail mix

¼ cup butter or
  margarine

2 tablespoons sugar

1 teaspoon ground
  cinnamon

1 cup bite-sized oat
  cereal squares

1 cup bite-sized wheat
  cereal squares

1 cup bite-sized rice
  cereal squares

¼ cup toasted slivered
  almonds

¾ cup raisins

1. Melt butter at HIGH (100%) 1½ minutes in large microwave-safe bowl. Add sugar and cinnamon; mix well. Add cereals and nuts; stir to coat.

2. Microwave at HIGH 2 minutes. Stir well. Microwave 2 minutes more; stir well. Add raisins. Microwave an additional 2 to 3 minutes, stirring well after 2 minutes. Spread on paper towels; mix will become crisp as it cools. Store tightly covered. *makes about 4 cups*

breakfast blossoms

1 (12-ounce) can
  buttermilk biscuits
  (10 biscuits)

¾ cup **SMUCKER'S®**
  Strawberry
  Preserves

¼ teaspoon ground
  cinnamon

¼ teaspoon ground
  nutmeg

Grease ten 2½- or 3-inch muffin cups. Separate dough into 10 biscuits. Separate each biscuit into 3 even sections or leaves. Stand 3 sections evenly around sides and bottom of cup, overlapping slightly. Press dough edges firmly together.

Combine preserves, cinnamon and nutmeg; place scant tablespoonful in center of each cup.

Bake at 375°F for 10 to 12 minutes or until lightly browned. Cool slightly before removing from pan. Serve warm. *makes 10 rolls*

strawberry muffins

1¼ cups all-purpose flour

2½ teaspoons baking
powder

½ teaspoon salt

1 cup uncooked old-
fashioned oats

½ cup sugar

1 cup milk

½ cup butter, melted

1 egg, beaten

1 teaspoon vanilla

1 cup chopped fresh
strawberries

Preheat oven to 425°F. Grease 12 (2½-inch) muffin cups; set aside.

Combine flour, baking powder and salt in large bowl. Stir in oats and sugar. Combine milk, butter, egg and vanilla in small bowl until well blended; stir into flour mixture just until moistened. Fold in strawberries. Spoon into prepared muffin cups, filling about two-thirds full.

Bake 15 to 18 minutes or until lightly browned and toothpick inserted in center comes out clean. Remove from pan. Cool on wire rack 10 minutes. Serve warm or cool completely.   *makes 12 muffins*

pumpkin bread

1 package (about
18 ounces) yellow
cake mix

⅓ cup GRANDMA'S®
Molasses (gold
label)

4 eggs

1 can (16 ounces) solid
pack pumpkin

1 teaspoon cinnamon

1 teaspoon nutmeg

⅓ cup nuts, chopped
(optional)

⅓ cup raisins (optional)

Preheat oven to 350°F. Grease two 9×5-inch loaf pans.

Combine all ingredients in a large bowl and mix well. Beat at medium speed 2 minutes. Pour into prepared pans. Bake 60 minutes or until toothpick inserted in center comes out clean.   *makes 2 loaves*

hint: Serve with cream cheese or preserves, or top with cream cheese frosting or ice cream.

apple cinnamon quesadillas

Spiced Yogurt Dipping Sauce (recipe follows)

1 medium McIntosh apple, cored and chopped

¾ cup no-sugar-added applesauce

⅛ teaspoon ground cinnamon

4 flour tortillas (6-inch)

¼ cup (1 ounce) shredded reduced-fat Cheddar cheese

Nonstick cooking spray

1. Prepare Spiced Yogurt Dipping Sauce. Set aside.

2. Combine apple, applesauce and cinnamon in small bowl; mix well.

3. Spoon half of apple mixture onto tortilla; sprinkle with half of cheese. Top with another tortilla. Repeat with remaining tortillas and apple mixture.

4. Spray large nonstick skillet with cooking spray; heat over medium heat until hot. Cook quesadillas, one at a time, about 2 minutes on each side or until golden brown. Cut each quesadilla into four wedges. Serve with Spiced Yogurt Dipping Sauce. *makes 4 servings*

spiced yogurt dipping sauce

½ cup vanilla low-fat yogurt

2 tablespoons no-sugar-added applesauce

Dash ground cinnamon

Combine yogurt, applesauce and cinnamon in small bowl; mix well. Refrigerate until ready to use.

34

ham and cheese corn muffins

1 package (8½ ounces) corn muffin mix

½ cup chopped deli ham

½ cup (2 ounces) shredded Swiss cheese

⅓ cup reduced-fat (2%) milk

1 egg

1 tablespoon Dijon mustard

1. Preheat oven to 400°F. Combine muffin mix, ham and cheese in medium bowl.

2. Combine milk, egg and mustard in 1-cup glass measure. Stir milk mixture into dry ingredients; mix just until moistened.

3. Fill 9 paper cup-lined 2¾-inch muffin cups two-thirds full with batter.

4. Bake 18 to 20 minutes or until light golden brown. Remove muffin pan to cooling rack. Let stand 5 minutes. Serve warm.

makes 9 muffins

serving suggestion: For added flavor, serve Ham and Cheese Corn Muffins with honey-flavored butter. To prepare, stir together equal amounts of honey and softened butter.

prep and cook time: 30 minutes

hearty banana carrot muffins

2 ripe, medium DOLE® Bananas

1 package (14 ounces) oat bran muffin mix

¾ teaspoon ground ginger

1 medium DOLE® Carrot, shredded (½ cup)

⅓ cup light molasses

⅓ cup DOLE® Raisins

¼ cup chopped almonds

• Mash bananas with fork. (1 cup)

• Combine muffin mix and ginger in large bowl. Add carrot, molasses, raisins and bananas. Stir just until moistened.

• Spoon batter into paper-lined muffin cups. Sprinkle tops with almonds.

• Bake at 425°F 12 to 14 minutes until browned.   *makes 12 muffins*

prep time: 20 minutes
bake time: 14 minutes

36

crispy's™ vanishing pancakes

2 cups all-purpose flour

1 tablespoon granulated sugar

1½ teaspoons baking powder

½ teaspoon baking soda

½ teaspoon salt

1 large egg

1½ cups buttermilk

¼ cup vegetable oil

¾ cup "M&M's"® Semi-Sweet Chocolate Mini Baking Bits, divided

Butter and maple syrup

Lightly grease and preheat griddle or large skillet over medium heat. In large bowl combine flour, sugar, baking powder, baking soda and salt. In medium bowl beat egg; gradually add buttermilk and oil until well blended. Blend egg mixture into flour mixture just until moistened. For each pancake, pour about ½ cup batter onto hot griddle. Sprinkle with about 1 tablespoon "M&M's"® Semi-Sweet Chocolate Mini Baking Bits. Cook until tops of pancakes appear dry; turn with spatula and cook 2 minutes or until golden brown. Serve with butter, maple syrup and remaining ¼ cup "M&M's"® Semi-Sweet Chocolate Mini Baking Bits.

makes 6 to 8 (5-inch) pancakes

spiced apple toast

1 tablespoon margarine

2 all-purpose apples, unpeeled, cored and thinly sliced

⅓ cup orange juice

4 teaspoons packed brown sugar

½ teaspoon ground cinnamon

4 slices whole wheat bread, toasted

2 teaspoons granulated sugar

Preheat oven to 450°F. Melt margarine in medium nonstick skillet. Add apples, orange juice, brown sugar and cinnamon; cook over medium-high heat about 4 minutes or until apples are tender, stirring occasionally. Drain; reserve cooking liquid. Cool apples 2 to 3 minutes. Place toast on lightly buttered baking sheet. Arrange apples, overlapping slices, in spiral design. Sprinkle ½ teaspoon granulated sugar over each slice. Bake 4 to 5 minutes or until bread is crisp. Drizzle reserved liquid over slices; serve immediately.

makes 4 servings

Favorite recipe from **The Sugar Association, Inc.**

french raisin toast

2 tablespoons
   granulated sugar

1 teaspoon ground
   cinnamon

4 eggs, lightly beaten

½ cup milk

8 slices raisin bread

4 tablespoons butter or
   margarine, divided

   Powdered sugar

1. Combine granulated sugar and cinnamon in wide shallow bowl. Beat in eggs and milk. Add bread; let stand to coat, then turn to coat other side.

2. Heat 2 tablespoons butter in large skillet over medium-low heat. Add 4 bread slices; cook until brown. Turn and cook other side. Remove; keep warm. Repeat with remaining butter and bread. Sprinkle with powdered sugar. Garnish as desired. Serve immediately.

makes 4 servings

tunnel of cheese muffins

2 cups biscuit mix

5 slices bacon, crisply
   cooked and
   crumbled

¾ cup milk

1 egg, beaten

12 (½-inch) cubes Swiss
   cheese

Stir together biscuit mix and bacon in medium bowl. Add milk and egg, stirring just to mix. Spoon half of batter into 12 buttered muffin pan cups. Press one cheese cube in each cup. Top with remaining batter, covering cheese completely. Bake in preheated 400°F oven 25 minutes or until golden. Serve hot.

makes 12 muffins

Favorite recipe from **Wisconsin Milk Marketing Board**

LUNCH

funny face sandwich melts

2 super-size English
    muffins, split and
    toasted

8 teaspoons *French's*®
    Honey Mustard

1 can (8 ounces)
    crushed pineapple,
    drained

8 ounces sliced smoked
    ham

4 slices Swiss cheese
    or white American
    cheese

1. Place English muffins, cut side up, on baking sheet. Spread each with *2 teaspoons* mustard. Arrange one-fourth of the pineapple, ham and cheese on top, dividing evenly.

2. Broil until cheese melts, about 1 minute. Decorate with mustard and assorted vegetables to create your own funny face.   *makes 4 servings*

tip: This sandwich is also easy to prepare in the toaster oven.

prep time: 10 minutes
cook time: 1 minute

peanut pitas

1 package (8 ounces) small pita breads, cut crosswise in half

16 teaspoons reduced-fat peanut butter

16 teaspoons strawberry spreadable fruit

1 large banana, peeled and thinly sliced (about 48 slices)

1. Spread inside of each pita half with 1 teaspoon each peanut butter and spreadable fruit.

2. Fill pita halves evenly with banana slices. Serve immediately.

makes 8 servings

honey bees: Substitute honey for spreadable fruit.

jolly jellies: Substitute any flavor jelly for spreadable fruit and thin apple slices for banana slices.

p. b. crunchers: Substitute reduced-fat mayonnaise for spreadable fruit and celery slices for banana slices.

fiesta chicken soup

6 TYSON® Individually Fresh Frozen® Boneless, Skinless Chicken Tenderloins

½ cup UNCLE BEN'S® Instant Rice

2 cans (14½ ounces each) low-sodium chicken broth

1 can (15 ounces) kidney beans, undrained

1 cup salsa

1 cup frozen whole-kernel corn

⅓ cup shredded Monterey Jack cheese

PREP: CLEAN: Wash hands. Remove protective ice glaze from frozen chicken by holding under cool running water 1 to 2 minutes. Cut chicken into 1-inch pieces. CLEAN: Wash hands.

COOK: In large saucepan, combine chicken, chicken broth, kidney beans, salsa and corn. Bring to a boil. Reduce heat and simmer, uncovered, 5 to 10 minutes or until internal juices of chicken run clear. (Or insert instant-read meat thermometer in thickest part of chicken. Temperature should read 170°F.) Stir in rice, cover and remove from heat. Let stand 5 minutes.

SERVE: Top individual servings of soup with cheese. Serve with fresh fruit and cornbread, if desired.

CHILL: Refrigerate leftovers immediately.

makes 4 servings

prep time: 10 minutes
cook time: 20 minutes

43

double-sauced chicken pizza bagels

1 whole bagel, split in half

4 tablespoons prepared pizza sauce

½ cup diced cooked chicken breast

¼ cup (1 ounce) shredded part-skim mozzarella cheese

2 teaspoons grated Parmesan cheese

1. Place bagel halves on microwavable plate.

2. Spoon 1 tablespoon pizza sauce onto each bagel half. Spread evenly using back of spoon.

3. Top each bagel half with ¼ cup chicken. Spoon 1 tablespoon pizza sauce over chicken on each bagel half.

4. Sprinkle 2 tablespoons mozzarella cheese over top of each bagel half.

5. Cover bagel halves loosely with waxed paper and microwave at HIGH 1 to 1½ minutes or until cheese melts.

6. Carefully remove waxed paper. Sprinkle each bagel half with 1 teaspoon Parmesan cheese. Let stand 1 minute before eating to cool slightly. (Bagels will be very hot.)

makes 2 servings (1 bagel half each)

tip: For crunchier "pizzas," toast bagels before adding toppings.

44

chunky potato bacon soup

- **1 package (32 ounces) frozen Southern-style hash brown potatoes, thawed**
- **1 quart milk**
- **1 can (10¾ ounces) condensed cream of celery soup**
- **1 cup (6 ounces) cubed processed cheese**
- **⅓ cup cooked chopped bacon (4 slices uncooked)**
- **1 tablespoon *French's*® Worcestershire Sauce**
- **1⅓ cups *French's*® *Taste Toppers*™ French Fried Onions**

1. Combine potatoes, milk, soup, cheese, bacon and Worcestershire in large saucepot. Heat to boiling over medium-high heat, stirring often.

2. Heat *Taste Toppers* in microwave on HIGH 2 minutes or until golden. Ladle soup into bowls. Sprinkle with *Taste Toppers*. Garnish with fresh minced parsley if desired.   *makes 6 servings*

prep time: 5 minutes
cook time: 10 minutes

Make soup more exciting by serving it in an edible bowl, such as a French roll or small round sourdough loaf. Simply slice a small piece from the top of the bread, then remove the center, leaving a 1-inch shell. Toast the bread bowls lightly before filling them with soup. These bowls are great for thicker soups and stews (such as chowders or chili), but they cannot be used to hold thin soups (such as chicken noodle).

crunchy turkey pita pockets

1 cup diced cooked turkey or chicken breast or reduced-sodium deli turkey breast

½ cup packaged cole slaw mix

½ cup dried cranberries

¼ cup shredded carrots

2 tablespoons reduced-fat or fat-free mayonnaise

1 tablespoon honey mustard

2 whole wheat pita breads

1. Combine turkey, cole slaw mix, cranberries, carrots, mayonnaise and mustard in small bowl; mix well.

2. Cut pita breads in half; fill with turkey mixture.

makes 2 servings

dizzy dogs

1 package (8 breadsticks or 11 ounces) refrigerated breadsticks

1 package (16 ounces) hot dogs

1 egg white, lightly beaten

Sesame and/or poppy seeds

Mustard, ketchup and barbecue sauce (optional)

1. Preheat oven to 375°F.

2. Using 1 breadstick for each, wrap hot dogs with dough in spiral pattern. Brush dough with beaten egg white; sprinkle with sesame and/or poppy seeds.

3. Bake 12 to 15 minutes or until light golden brown. Serve with condiments for dipping, if desired.

makes 8 hot dogs

kids' wrap

4 teaspoons Dijon honey mustard

2 (8-inch) fat-free flour tortillas

2 slices reduced-fat American cheese, torn into halves

4 ounces fat-free oven-roasted turkey breast

½ cup shredded carrots (about 1 medium)

3 romaine lettuce leaves, washed and torn into bite-size pieces

1. Spread 2 teaspoons mustard evenly over one tortilla.

2. Top with 2 cheese halves, half of turkey, half of shredded carrots and half of torn lettuce.

3. Roll up tortilla and cut in half. Repeat with remaining ingredients.

makes 2 servings

super spread sandwich stars

1 Red or Golden Delicious apple, peeled, cored and coarsely chopped

1 cup roasted peanuts

⅓ cup honey

1 tablespoon lemon juice

1 teaspoon ground cinnamon

Sliced sandwich bread

For Super Spread, place chopped apple, peanuts, honey, lemon juice and cinnamon in food processor or blender. Pulse food processor several times until ingredients start to blend, occasionally scraping down the sides with rubber spatula. Process 1 to 2 minutes until mixture is smooth and spreadable.

For Sandwich Stars, use butter knife to spread about 1 tablespoon Super Spread on 2 slices of bread. Stack them together, spread side up. Top with third slice bread. Place cookie cutter on top of sandwich; press down firmly and evenly. Leaving cookie cutter in place, remove excess trimmings with your fingers or a butter knife. Remove cookie cutter. *makes 1¼ cups spread (enough for about 10 sandwiches)*

Favorite recipe from **Texas Peanut Producers Board**

48

bologna "happy faces"

4 slices whole wheat or rye bread

1 cup prepared oil and vinegar based coleslaw

8 ounces HEBREW NATIONAL® Sliced Lean Beef Bologna or Lean Beef Salami

4 large pimiento-stuffed green olives

HEBREW NATIONAL® Deli Mustard

For each sandwich, spread 1 bread slice with 3 tablespoons coleslaw; top with 5 slices bologna. Cut olives in half crosswise; place over bologna for "eyes." Draw smiley "mouth" with mustard. Drop 1 tablespoon coleslaw at top of face for "hair."

makes 4 open-faced sandwiches

cheeseburger calzones

1 pound ground beef

1 medium onion, chopped

½ teaspoon salt

1 jar (26 to 28 ounces) RAGÚ® Hearty Robusto!™ Pasta Sauce

1 jar (8 ounces) marinated mushrooms, drained and chopped (optional)

1 cup shredded Cheddar cheese (about 4 ounces)

1 package (2 pounds) frozen pizza dough, thawed

1. Preheat oven to 375°F. In 12-inch skillet, brown ground beef with onion and salt over medium-high heat; drain. Stir in 1 cup Ragú® Hearty Robusto! Pasta Sauce, mushrooms and cheese.

2. On floured board, cut each pound of dough into 4 pieces; press to form 6-inch circles. Spread ½ cup beef mixture on each dough circle; fold over and pinch edges to close.

3. With large spatula, gently arrange on cookie sheets. Bake 25 minutes or until golden. Serve with remaining sauce, heated.

makes 8 servings

prep time: 15 minutes
cook time: 25 minutes

50

pizza rollers

1 package (10 ounces)
  refrigerated pizza
  dough
½ cup pizza sauce
18 slices turkey
  pepperoni
6 sticks mozzarella
  cheese

1. Preheat oven to 425°F. Coat baking sheet with nonstick cooking spray.

2. Roll out pizza dough on baking sheet to form 12×9-inch rectangle. Cut pizza dough into 6 (4½×4-inch) rectangles. Spread about 1 tablespoon sauce over center third of each rectangle. Top with 3 slices pepperoni and stick of mozzarella cheese. Bring ends of dough together over cheese, pinching to seal. Place, seam side down, on prepared baking sheet.

3. Bake in center of oven 10 minutes or until golden brown.

makes 6 servings

lunch box handwiches

1 package BOB EVANS®
  Frozen White Dinner
  Roll Dough
1 pound BOB EVANS®
  Italian Roll Sausage
⅓ cup tomato sauce
½ cup (2 ounces)
  shredded
  mozzarella or
  Cheddar cheese
1 egg yolk
1 tablespoon water

Thaw dough at room temperature 45 minutes to 1 hour. Allow dough to rise according to package directions. Preheat oven to 375°F. Crumble and cook sausage in medium skillet until browned. Drain off any drippings; let cool. Punch down dough; press each piece into 5- to 6-inch circle. Place about ⅓ cup cooked sausage, 2 teaspoons sauce and 1 tablespoon cheese on each circle; press filling down to flatten. Bring edges up over filling and seal edges to form a ball. Place seam sides down on greased baking sheet. Beat egg yolk and water; brush tops of dough with mixture. Bake 15 to 20 minutes or until golden brown. Serve warm, or cool, wrap and freeze to reheat and serve another time. Refrigerate leftovers. *makes 7 handwiches*

serving suggestion: Serve handwiches with a dipping sauce, such as tomato, pizza or spaghetti sauce.

chicken nuggets with barbecue dipping sauce

1 pound boneless
   skinless chicken
   breasts
¼ cup all-purpose flour
¼ teaspoon salt
   (optional)
   Black pepper to taste
2 cups crushed
   reduced-fat baked
   cheese crackers
1 teaspoon dried
   oregano leaves
1 egg white
1 tablespoon water
3 tablespoons barbecue
   sauce
2 tablespoons no-sugar-
   added peach or
   apricot jam

1. Preheat oven to 400°F. Rinse chicken. Pat dry with paper towels. Cut into 1-inch chunks.

2. Place flour, salt and pepper in resealable plastic food storage bag. Combine cracker crumbs and oregano in shallow bowl. Whisk together egg white and water in small bowl.

3. Place 6 or 8 chicken pieces in bag with flour mixture; seal bag. Shake bag until chicken is well coated. Remove chicken from bag, shaking off excess flour. Dip chicken pieces into egg white mixture, coating all sides. Roll in crumb mixture. Place in shallow baking pan. Repeat with remaining chicken pieces. Bake 10 to 13 minutes or until golden brown.

4. Meanwhile, stir together barbecue sauce and jam in small saucepan. Cook and stir over low heat until heated through. (If freezing nuggets, do not prepare dipping sauce at this time.) Serve chicken nuggets with dipping sauce or follow directions for freezing and reheating.

makes 8 servings

note: To freeze chicken nuggets, cool 5 minutes on baking sheet. Wrap chicken in plastic wrap, making packages of 4 to 5 nuggets each. Place packages in freezer container or plastic freezer bag. Freeze. To reheat nuggets, preheat oven to 325°F. Unwrap nuggets. Place nuggets on ungreased baking sheet. Bake for 13 to 15 minutes or until hot. Or, place 4 to 5 nuggets on microwavable plate. Heat on DEFROST (30% power) for 2½ to 3½ minutes or until hot, turning once.

For each serving, stir together about 1½ teaspoons barbecue sauce and ½ teaspoon jam in small microwavable dish. Heat on HIGH 10 to 15 seconds or until hot.

grilled cheese & turkey shapes

8 teaspoons *French's*® Mustard, any flavor

8 slices seedless rye or sourdough bread

8 slices deli roast turkey

4 slices American cheese

2 tablespoons butter or margarine, softened

1. Spread *1 teaspoon* mustard on each slice of bread. Arrange turkey and cheese on half of the bread slices, dividing evenly. Cover with top halves of bread.

2. Cut out sandwich shapes using choice of cookie cutters. Place cookie cutter on top of sandwich; press down firmly. Remove excess trimmings.

3. Spread butter on both sides of bread. Heat large nonstick skillet over medium heat. Cook sandwiches 1 minute per side or until bread is golden and cheese melts. *makes 4 sandwiches*

tip: Use 2½-inch star, heart, teddy-bear or flower-shaped cookie cutters.

prep time: 15 minutes
cook time: 2 minutes

Kids love these sandwiches, so if you find that you're serving them often, try varying the sandwich ingredients from time to time. Substitute deli sliced ham for turkey, and use Cheddar, Swiss or mozzarella cheese instead of American cheese for a change of pace.

56

quick and easy italian sandwich

1 tablespoon olive or vegetable oil

½ pound mild Italian sausage, casing removed, sliced ½ inch thick

1 can (14.5 ounces) CONTADINA® Recipe Ready Diced Tomatoes with Italian Herbs, undrained

½ cup sliced green bell pepper

6 sandwich-size English muffins, split, toasted

¼ cup (1 ounce) shredded Parmesan cheese, divided

1. Heat oil in medium skillet. Add sausage; cook 3 to 4 minutes or until no longer pink in center, stirring occasionally. Drain.

2. Add undrained tomatoes and bell pepper; simmer, uncovered, 5 minutes, stirring occasionally.

3. Spread ½ cup meat mixture on each of 6 muffin halves; sprinkle with Parmesan cheese. Top with remaining muffin halves.

makes 6 servings

It's more economical to purchase a chunk of cheese and grate it yourself than to buy already grated cheese. (It also lasts longer.) Hard cheeses like Parmesan can be grated on a flat metal grater with small holes, a box grater or a hand-held rotary grater.

piñata twirls

- **1 cup UNCLE BEN'S® ORIGINAL CONVERTED® Brand Rice**
- **1 package (1 pound) TYSON® Fresh Ground Chicken**
- **1 jar (16 ounces) chunky salsa**
- **1½ cups corn (frozen, fresh or canned, drained)**
- **16 (8-inch) whole wheat flour tortillas, warmed**
- **1 cup shredded Colby-Jack cheese**

COOK: Prepare rice according to package directions. CLEAN: Wash hands. In large nonstick skillet, cook chicken over medium-high heat 6 to 8 minutes or until no longer pink. Stir in salsa, cooked rice and corn. Simmer 5 minutes or until liquid is absorbed. Spoon ⅓ cup mixture onto warm tortilla; top with 1 tablespoon cheese. Tightly roll tortilla to serve.

SERVE: Serve with chips and salsa, if desired.

CHILL: Refrigerate leftovers immediately.

makes 8 servings

prep time: none
cook time: 35 minutes

corn dogs

8 hot dogs

8 wooden craft sticks

1 package (about 16 ounces) refrigerated grand-size corn biscuits

⅓ cup *French's*® Classic Yellow® Mustard

8 slices American cheese, cut in half

1. Preheat oven to 350°F. Insert 1 wooden craft stick halfway into each hot dog; set aside.

2. Separate biscuits. On floured board, press or roll each biscuit into a 7×4-inch oval. Spread *2 teaspoons* mustard lengthwise down center of each biscuit. Top each with 2 pieces of cheese. Place hot dog in center of biscuit. Fold top of dough over end of hot dog. Fold sides towards center enclosing hot dog. Pinch edges to seal.

3. Place corn dogs, seam-side down, on greased baking sheet. Bake 20 to 25 minutes or until golden brown. Cool slightly before serving.

makes 8 servings

tip: Corn dogs may be made without wooden craft sticks.

prep time: 15 minutes
cook time: 20 minutes

cheeseburger soup

½ pound ground beef

3½ cups water

½ cup cherry tomato halves or chopped tomato

1 pouch LIPTON® Soup Secrets Ring-O-Noodle Soup Mix with Real Chicken Broth

4 ounces Cheddar cheese, shredded

Shape ground beef into 16 mini burgers.

In large saucepan, thoroughly brown burgers; drain. Add water, tomatoes and soup mix; bring to a boil. Reduce heat and simmer uncovered, stirring occasionally, 5 minutes or until burgers are cooked and noodles are tender. Stir in cheese.

makes about 4 (1-cup) servings

rock 'n' rollers

4 (6- to 7-inch) flour
   tortillas

4 ounces reduced-fat
   cream cheese,
   softened

⅓ cup peach preserves

1 cup (4 ounces)
   shredded Cheddar
   cheese

½ cup packed washed
   fresh spinach leaves

3 ounces thinly sliced
   regular or smoked
   turkey breast

1. Spread each tortilla evenly with 1 ounce cream cheese; cover with thin layer of preserves. Sprinkle with Cheddar cheese.

2. Arrange spinach leaves and turkey over Cheddar cheese. Roll up tortillas; trim ends. Cover and refrigerate until ready to serve.

3. Cut "rollers" crosswise in half or diagonally into 1-inch pieces.

makes 8 servings

sassy salsa rollers: Substitute salsa for peach preserves and shredded iceberg lettuce for spinach leaves.

ham 'n' apple rollers: Omit peach preserves and spinach leaves. Substitute lean ham slices for turkey. Spread tortillas with cream cheese as directed; sprinkle with Cheddar cheese. Top each tortilla with about 2 tablespoons finely chopped apple and 2 ham slices; roll up. Continue as directed.

wedgies: Prepare Rock 'n' Rollers or any variation as directed, but do not roll up. Top with a second tortilla; cut into wedges.

sub on the run

2 hard rolls, split into halves

4 tomato slices

14 turkey pepperoni slices

2 ounces fat-free oven-roasted turkey breast

¼ cup (1 ounce) shredded part-skim mozzarella or reduced-fat sharp Cheddar cheese

1 cup packaged coleslaw mix or shredded lettuce

¼ medium green bell pepper, thinly sliced (optional)

2 tablespoons prepared fat-free Italian salad dressing

Top each of the two bottom halves of rolls with 2 tomato slices, 7 pepperoni slices, half of turkey, 2 tablespoons cheese, ½ cup coleslaw mix and half of bell pepper slices, if desired. Drizzle with salad dressing. Top with roll tops. Cut into halves, if desired.

makes 2 servings

Subs make great party food for kids! To make a party-sized sub, purchase long French or Italian breads at the supermarket and inrease the quantity of sandwich ingredients according to how many kids you'll be serving. Or, purchase round loaves of bread and cut the sandwich into wedges instead.

64

tuna monte cristo sandwiches

4 thin slices (2 ounces) Cheddar cheese

4 oval slices sourdough or challah (egg) bread

½ pound deli tuna salad

1 egg, beaten

¼ cup milk

2 tablespoons butter or margarine

1. Place 1 slice cheese on each bread slice. Spread tuna salad evenly over two slices of cheese-topped bread. Close sandwich with remaining bread.

2. Combine egg and milk in shallow bowl. Dip sandwiches in egg mixture, turning to coat well.

3. Melt butter in large nonstick skillet over medium heat. Add sandwiches; cook 4 to 5 minutes per side or until golden brown and cheese is melted.

makes 2 servings

serving suggestion: Serve with a chilled fruit salad.

prep and cook time: 20 minutes

zesty chicken & vegetable soup

½ pound boneless skinless chicken breasts, cut into very thin strips

1 to 2 tablespoons *Frank's® RedHot®* Sauce

4 cups chicken broth

1 package (16 ounces) frozen stir-fry vegetables

1 cup angel hair pasta, broken into 2-inch lengths *or* fine egg noodles

1 green onion, thinly sliced

1. Combine chicken and **RedHot** Sauce in medium bowl; set aside.

2. Heat broth to boiling in large saucepan over medium-high heat. Add vegetables and noodles; return to boiling. Cook 2 minutes. Stir in chicken mixture and green onion. Cook 1 minute or until chicken is no longer pink.

makes 4 to 6 servings

tip: For a change of pace, substitute 6 prepared frozen pot stickers for the pasta. Add to broth in step 2 and boil until tender.

prep time: 5 minutes
cook time: about 8 minutes

tuna monte cristo sandwich

rainbow spirals

4 (10-inch) flour tortillas (assorted flavors and colors)

4 tablespoons *French's*® Mustard (any flavor)

½ pound (about 8 slices) thinly sliced deli roast beef, bologna or turkey

8 slices American, provolone or Muenster cheese

Fancy party toothpicks

1. Spread each tortilla with *1 tablespoon* mustard. Layer with meat and cheese, dividing evenly.

2. Roll-up jelly-roll style; secure with toothpicks and cut into thirds. Arrange on platter.

makes 4 to 6 servings

prep time: 10 minutes

quick corn bread with chilies 'n' cheese

1 package (12 to 16 ounces) corn bread or corn muffin mix

1 cup (4 ounces) shredded Monterey Jack cheese

1 can (4 ounces) chopped green chilies, drained

1 envelope LIPTON® RECIPE SECRETS® Vegetable Soup Mix

Prepare corn bread mix according to package directions; stir in ½ cup cheese, chilies and vegetable soup mix. Pour batter into lightly greased 8-inch baking pan; bake as directed. While warm, top with remaining cheese. Cool completely on wire rack. To serve, cut into squares.

makes 16 servings

68

SNACKS

perfect pita pizzas

2 whole wheat or white pita bread rounds

½ cup spaghetti or pizza sauce

¾ cup (3 ounces) shredded part-skim mozzarella cheese

1 small zucchini, sliced ¼ inch thick

½ small carrot, peeled and sliced

2 cherry tomatoes, halved

¼ small green bell pepper, sliced

1. Preheat oven to 375°F. Line baking sheet with foil; set aside.

2. Using small scissors, carefully split each pita bread round around edge; separate to form 2 rounds.

3. Place rounds, rough sides up, on prepared baking sheet. Bake 5 minutes.

4. Spread 2 tablespoons spaghetti sauce onto each round; sprinkle with cheese. Decorate with vegetables to create faces. Bake 10 to 12 minutes or until cheese melts. *makes 4 servings*

pepperoni pita pizzas: Prepare pita rounds, partially bake and top with spaghetti sauce and cheese as directed. Place 2 small pepperoni slices on each pizza for eyes. Decorate with cut-up fresh vegetables for rest of face. Continue to bake as directed.

festive franks

1 can (8 ounces) reduced-fat crescent roll dough

5½ teaspoons barbecue sauce

⅓ cup finely shredded reduced-fat sharp Cheddar cheese

8 fat-free hot dogs

¼ teaspoon poppy seeds (optional)

Additional barbecue sauce (optional)

1. Preheat oven to 350°F. Spray large baking sheet with nonstick cooking spray; set aside.

2. Unroll dough and separate into 8 triangles. Cut each triangle in half lengthwise to make 2 triangles. Lightly spread barbecue sauce over each triangle. Sprinkle with cheese.

3. Cut each hot dog in half; trim off rounded ends. Place one hot dog piece at large end of one dough triangle. Roll up jelly-roll style from wide end. Place point-side down on prepared baking sheet. Sprinkle with poppy seeds, if desired. Repeat with remaining hot dog pieces and dough.

4. Bake 13 minutes or until dough is golden brown. Cool 1 to 2 minutes on baking sheet. Serve with additional barbecue sauce for dipping, if desired.

makes 16 servings

berry striped pops

2 cups strawberries

¾ cup honey,* divided

6 kiwifruit, peeled and sliced

2 cups sliced peaches

12 (3-ounce) paper cups or popsicle molds

12 popsicle sticks

*Honey should not be fed to infants under one year of age. Honey is a safe and wholesome food for older children and adults.

Purée strawberries with ¼ cup honey in blender or food processor. Divide mixture evenly between 12 cups or popsicle molds. Freeze about 30 minutes or until firm. Meanwhile, rinse processor; purée kiwifruit with ¼ cup honey. Repeat process with peaches and remaining ¼ cup honey. When strawberry layer is firm, pour kiwifruit purée into molds. Insert popsicle sticks and freeze about 30 minutes or until firm. Pour peach purée into molds and freeze until firm and ready to serve.

makes 12 servings

Favorite recipe from **National Honey Board**

bread pudding snacks

1¼ cups reduced-fat
(2%) milk

½ cup egg substitute

⅓ cup sugar

1 teaspoon vanilla

⅛ teaspoon salt

⅛ teaspoon ground
nutmeg (optional)

4 cups (½-inch)
cinnamon or
cinnamon-raisin
bread cubes (about
6 bread slices)

1 tablespoon margarine
or butter, melted

1. Combine milk, egg substitute, sugar, vanilla, salt and nutmeg in medium bowl; mix well. Add bread; mix until well moistened. Let stand at room temperature 15 minutes.

2. Preheat oven to 350°F. Line 12 medium-sized muffin cups with paper liners.

3. Spoon bread mixture evenly into prepared cups; drizzle evenly with margarine.

4. Bake 30 to 35 minutes or until snacks are puffed and golden brown. Remove to wire rack to cool completely. *makes 12 servings*

note: Snacks will puff up in the oven and fall slightly upon cooling.

banana tot pops

3 firm, medium DOLE®
Bananas

6 large wooden sticks

½ cup raspberry or other
flavored yogurt

1 jar (1¾ ounces)
chocolate or
rainbow sprinkles

• Cut each banana crosswise in half. Insert wooden stick into each half.

• Pour yogurt into small bowl. Hold banana pop over bowl; spoon yogurt to cover all sides of banana. Allow excess yogurt to drip into bowl. Sprinkle candies over yogurt.

• Place pops on wax paper lined tray. Freeze 2 hours.

makes 6 servings

prep time: 20 minutes
freeze time: 2 hours

cocoa snackin' jacks

1 (3-ounce) bag ORVILLE REDENBACHER'S® Microwave Popping Corn, popped according to package instructions

½ cup crumbled reduced fat chocolate cookies

½ cup granulated sugar

½ cup firmly packed brown sugar

¼ cup light corn syrup

2 tablespoons reduced fat margarine

1 tablespoon water

¼ teaspoon cream of tartar

1 (.53-oz) package SWISS MISS® Fat Free Hot Cocoa Mix

1 teaspoon baking soda

1. In large bowl, combine Orville Redenbacher's Popped Corn and cookies; set aside.

2. In medium saucepan, combine sugars, syrup, margarine, water and cream of tartar.

3. Bring to a boil and stir constantly until thermometer reaches 260°F. Remove from heat.

4. Quickly add Swiss Miss Cocoa and baking soda; stir thoroughly.

5. Working quickly, pour mixture over popcorn and cookie mixture. Gently toss to coat.

6. Spread mixture onto waxed paper to cool and harden. Break into pieces.   *makes 16 (1-ounce) servings*

To soften brown sugar that has hardened, place 1 cup of brown sugar in a microwavable bowl and cover with plastic wrap. Heat at High 30 to 45 seconds; stir and repeat if necessary. Watch the brown sugar carefully to make sure it doesn't melt.

cheddary pull apart bread

- 1 round loaf corn or sourdough bread (1 pound)*
- ½ cup (1 stick) butter or margarine, melted
- ¼ cup *French's®* Classic Yellow® Mustard
- ½ teaspoon chili powder
- ½ teaspoon seasoned salt
- ¼ teaspoon garlic powder
- 1 cup (4 ounces) shredded Cheddar cheese

You may substitute one 12-inch loaf Italian bread for the corn bread.

Cut bread into 1-inch slices, cutting about ⅔ of the way down through loaf. (Do not cut through bottom crust.) Turn bread ¼ turn and cut across slices in similar fashion. Combine butter, mustard and seasonings in small bowl until blended. Brush cut surfaces of bread with butter mixture. Spread bread "sticks" apart and sprinkle cheese inside. Wrap loaf in foil.

Place packet on grid. Cook over medium coals about 30 minutes or until bread is toasted and cheese melts. Pull bread "sticks" apart to serve.

makes about 8 servings

prep time: 15 minutes
cook time: 30 minutes

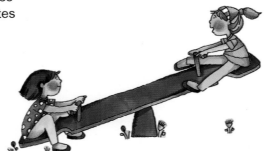

pepperoni pizza dip

- 1 cup RAGÚ® Old World Style® Pasta Sauce
- 1 cup RAGÚ® Cheese Creations!® Classic Alfredo Sauce
- 1 cup shredded mozzarella cheese (about 4 ounces)
- ¼ to ½ cup finely chopped pepperoni

1. In 2-quart saucepan, heat Ragú Pasta Sauces, cheese and pepperoni, stirring occasionally, 10 minutes or until cheese is melted.

2. Pour into 1½-quart casserole or serving dish and serve, if desired, with breadsticks, sliced Italian bread or crackers.

makes 3½ cups dip

prep time: 5 minutes
cook time: 10 minutes

kids' quesadillas

8 slices American
cheese

8 (10-inch) flour tortillas

6 tablespoons *French's*®
Honey Mustard

½ pound thinly sliced
deli turkey

2 tablespoons melted
butter

¼ teaspoon paprika

1. To prepare 1 quesadilla, arrange 2 slices of cheese on 1 tortilla. Top with one-fourth of the turkey. Spread with *1½ tablespoons* mustard, then top with another tortilla. Prepare 3 more quesadillas with remaining ingredients.

2. Combine butter and paprika. Brush one side of tortilla with butter mixture. Preheat 12-inch nonstick skillet over medium-high heat. Arrange tortilla butter side down and cook 2 minutes. Brush tortilla with butter mixture and turn over. Cook 1½ minutes or until golden brown. Repeat with remaining three quesadillas.

3. Slice into wedges before serving.   *makes 4 servings*

prep time: 5 minutes
cook time: 15 minutes

creamy hot chocolate

1 (14-ounce) can
EAGLE® BRAND
Sweetened
Condensed Milk
(NOT evaporated
milk)

½ cup unsweetened
cocoa

1½ teaspoons vanilla
extract

⅛ teaspoon salt

6½ cups hot water
Marshmallows
(optional)

1. In large saucepan over medium heat, combine Eagle Brand, cocoa, vanilla and salt; mix well.

2. Slowly stir in water. Heat through, stirring occasionally. Do not boil. Top with marshmallows, if desired. Store covered in refrigerator.

makes about 2 quarts

microwave directions: In 2-quart glass measure, combine all ingredients except marshmallows. Microwave on 100% power (HIGH) 8 to 10 minutes, stirring every 3 minutes. Top with marshmallows, if desired. Store covered in refrigerator.

tip: Hot chocolate can be stored in refrigerator up to 5 days. Mix well and reheat before serving.

prep time: 8 to 10 minutes

78

one potato, two potato

Nonstick cooking spray

2 medium baking potatoes, cut lengthwise into 4 wedges

Salt

½ cup unseasoned dry bread crumbs

2 tablespoons grated Parmesan cheese (optional)

1½ teaspoons dried oregano leaves, dill weed, Italian herbs or paprika

Spicy brown or honey mustard, ketchup or reduced-fat sour cream

1. Preheat oven to 425°F. Spray baking sheet with nonstick cooking spray; set aside.

2. Spray cut sides of potatoes generously with cooking spray; sprinkle lightly with salt.

3. Combine bread crumbs, Parmesan cheese and desired herb in shallow dish. Add potatoes; toss lightly until potatoes are generously coated with crumb mixture. Place on prepared baking sheet.

4. Bake potatoes until browned and tender, about 20 minutes. Serve warm as dippers with mustard. *makes 4 servings*

potato sweets: Omit Parmesan cheese, herbs and mustard. Substitute sweet potatoes for baking potatoes. Cut and spray potatoes as directed; coat generously with desired amount of cinnamon-sugar. Bake as directed. Serve warm as dippers with peach or pineapple preserves or honey mustard.

peanut butter-pineapple celery sticks

½ cup low-fat (1%) cottage cheese

½ cup reduced-fat peanut butter

½ cup crushed pineapple in juice, drained

12 (3-inch-long) celery sticks

Combine cottage cheese and peanut butter in food processor. Blend until smooth. Stir in pineapple. Stuff celery sticks with mixture. *makes 4 servings*

variation: Substitute 2 medium apples, sliced, for celery.

80

cinnamon-raisin roll-ups

- **4 ounces reduced-fat cream cheese, softened**
- **½ cup shredded carrot**
- **¼ cup raisins**
- **1 tablespoon honey**
- **¼ teaspoon ground cinnamon**
- **4 (7- to 8-inch) whole wheat or regular flour tortillas**
- **8 thin apple wedges**

1. Combine cream cheese, carrot, raisins, honey and cinnamon in small bowl; mix well.

2. Spread tortillas evenly with cream cheese mixture, leaving ½-inch border around edge of each tortilla. Place 2 apple wedges down center of each tortilla; roll up. Wrap in plastic wrap. Refrigerate until ready to serve or pack in lunch box.

makes 4 servings

cook's tip: For extra convenience, prepare roll-ups the night before. In the morning, pack roll-up in lunch box along with a frozen juice box. The juice box will be thawed by lunchtime and will keep the snack cold in the meantime!

tuna 'n' celery sticks

- **4 ounces cream cheese, softened**
- **3 tablespoons plain yogurt or mayonnaise**
- **1½ teaspoons dried basil**
- **1 can (12 ounces) STARKIST® Solid White or Chunk Light Tuna, drained and flaked**
- **½ cup finely grated carrot or zucchini**
- **½ cup finely shredded Cheddar cheese**
- **2 teaspoons instant minced onion**
- **10 to 12 celery stalks, cleaned**

In large bowl, mix together cream cheese, yogurt and basil until smooth. Add tuna, carrot, Cheddar cheese and onion; mix well. Spread mixture into celery stalks; cut into fourths.

makes 40 servings

prep time: 10 minutes

herb cheese twists

2 tablespoons butter or margarine

¼ cup grated Parmesan cheese

1 teaspoon dried parsley flakes

1 teaspoon dried basil leaves

1 can (7½ ounces) refrigerated buttermilk biscuits

1. Preheat oven to 400°F. Microwave butter in small bowl at 50% power just until melted; cool slightly. Stir in cheese, parsley and basil. Set aside.

2. Pat each biscuit into 5×2-inch rectangle. Spread 1 teaspoon of butter mixture on each rectangle; cut each in half lengthwise. Twist each strip 3 or 4 times. Place on lightly greased baking sheet. Bake 8 to 10 minutes or until golden brown.   *makes 5 servings*

cut the time: Butter mixture can be spread on ready-to-bake bread sticks and baked according to package directions.

prep and cook time: 20 minutes

chocolate-peanut butter-apple treats

½ (8-ounce package) fat-free or reduced-fat cream cheese, softened

¼ cup reduced-fat chunky peanut butter

2 tablespoons mini chocolate chips

2 large apples

1. Combine cream cheese, peanut butter and chocolate chips in small bowl; mix well.

2. Cut each apple into 12 wedges; discard stems and seeds. Spread about 1½ teaspoons of the mixture over each apple slice.
makes 8 servings (4 apple wedges and 1½ teaspoons spread)

84

nachos à la ortega®

1¾ cups (1-pound can) ORTEGA® Refried Beans, warmed

4 cups (4 ounces) baked tortilla chips

1½ cups (6 ounces) shredded Monterey Jack cheese

2 tablespoons ORTEGA® Sliced Jalapeños

ORTEGA® Thick & Chunky Salsa, (optional)

Sour cream (optional)

Additional topping suggestions: guacamole, sliced ripe olives, chopped green onions, chopped fresh cilantro (optional)

PREHEAT broiler.

SPREAD beans over bottom of large ovenproof platter or 15×10-inch jelly-roll pan. Arrange chips over beans. Top with cheese and jalapeños.

BROIL for 1 to 1½ minutes or until cheese is melted. Top with salsa and sour cream.

makes 4 to 6 servings

Refried beans are made with red beans or pinto beans that are mashed and then fried (only once). They are often prepared with lard or beef flavoring, but vegetarian versions are also available, as well as flavored and fat-free varieties.

86

purple cow jumped over the moon

3 cups vanilla nonfat frozen yogurt

1 cup reduced-fat (2%) milk

½ cup thawed frozen grape juice concentrate (undiluted)

1½ teaspoons lemon juice

Place yogurt, milk, grape juice concentrate and lemon juice in food processor or blender container; process until smooth. Serve immediately. *makes 8 (½-cup) servings*

razzmatazz shake: Place 1 quart vanilla nonfat frozen yogurt, 1 cup vanilla nonfat yogurt and ¼ cup fat-free chocolate syrup in food processor or blender container; process until smooth. Pour ½ of mixture evenly into 12 glasses; top with ½ of (12-ounce) can root beer. Fill glasses equally with remaining yogurt mixture; top with remaining root beer. Makes 12 (⅔-cup) servings.

sunshine shake: Place 1 quart vanilla nonfat frozen yogurt, 1⅓ cups orange juice, 1 cup fresh or thawed frozen raspberries and 1 teaspoon sugar in food processor or blender container; process until smooth. Pour into 10 glasses; sprinkle with ground nutmeg. Makes 10 (½-cup) servings.

taco bread

1 loaf frozen bread dough, thawed

1½ cups (6 ounces) shredded cheddar cheese

1 package (1.0 ounce) LAWRY'S® Taco Spices & Seasonings

3 tablespoons butter or margarine, melted

On baking sheet, stretch dough into 14×8-inch rectangle. Sprinkle with cheese and Taco Seasoning Mix; drizzle with margarine. Roll up jelly roll fashion (lengthwise); place seam side down on baking sheet. Bake, uncovered, in 350°F oven 20 to 25 minutes until golden brown. *makes 6 servings*

serving suggestions: Slice bread when cooled and serve as a spicy addition to hearty soups.

honey popcorn clusters

Vegetable cooking spray

6 cups air-popped popcorn

⅔ cup DOLE® Golden or Seedless Raisins

½ cup DOLE® Chopped Dates or Pitted Dates, chopped

⅓ cup almonds (optional)

⅓ cup packed brown sugar

¼ cup honey

2 tablespoons margarine

¼ teaspoon baking soda

• Line bottom and sides of 13×9-inch baking pan with large sheet of aluminum foil. Spray foil with vegetable cooking spray.

• Stir together popcorn, raisins, dates and almonds in foil-lined pan.

• Combine brown sugar, honey and margarine in small saucepan. Bring to boil over medium heat, stirring constantly; reduce heat to low. Cook 5 minutes. *Do not stir.* Remove from heat.

• Stir in baking soda. Pour evenly over popcorn mixture, stirring quickly to coat mixture evenly.

• Bake at 300°F 12 to 15 minutes or until mixture is lightly browned, stirring once halfway through baking time.

• Lift foil from pan; place on cooling rack. Cool popcorn mixture completely; break into clusters. Popcorn clusters can be stored in airtight container up to 1 week.

makes 7 cups

prep time: 20 minutes
bake time: 15 minutes

stuffed bundles

1 package (10 ounces) refrigerated pizza dough

2 ounces lean ham or turkey ham, chopped

½ cup (2 ounces) shredded reduced-fat sharp Cheddar cheese

1. Preheat oven to 425°F. Coat nonstick 12-cup muffin pan with nonstick cooking spray.

2. Unroll dough on flat surface; cut into 12 pieces, about 4×3 inch rectangles.

3. Divide ham and cheese between dough rectangles. Bring corners of dough together, pinching to seal. Place, smooth side up, in prepared muffin cups.

4. Bake 10 to 12 minutes or until golden.

makes 12 servings

teddy bear party mix

4 cups crisp cinnamon
graham cereal

2 cups honey flavored
teddy-shaped
graham snacks

1 can (1½ ounces)
French's® Potato
Sticks

3 tablespoons melted
unsalted butter

2 tablespoons *French's*®
Worcestershire
Sauce

1 tablespoon packed
brown sugar

¼ teaspoon ground
cinnamon

1 cup sweetened dried
cranberries or
raisins

½ cup chocolate, peanut
butter or carob
chips

1. Preheat oven to 350°F. Lightly spray jelly-roll pan with nonstick cooking spray. Combine cereal, graham snacks and potato sticks in large bowl.

2. Combine butter, Worcestershire, sugar and cinnamon in small bowl; toss with cereal mixture. Transfer to prepared pan. Bake 12 minutes. Cool completely.

3. Stir in dried cranberries and chips. Store in an airtight container.

makes about 7 cups

prep time: 5 minutes
cook time: 12 minutes

pizza snack cups

1 can (12 ounces)
    refrigerated biscuits
    (10 biscuits)
½ pound ground beef
1 jar (14 ounces) RAGÚ®
    Pizza Quick® Sauce
½ cup shredded
    mozzarella cheese
    (about 2 ounces)

1. Preheat oven to 375°F. In 12-cup muffin pan, evenly press each biscuit in bottom and up side of each cup; chill until ready to fill.

2. In 10-inch skillet, brown ground beef over medium-high heat; drain. Stir in Ragú Pizza Quick Sauce and heat through.

3. Evenly spoon beef mixture into prepared muffin cups. Bake 15 minutes. Sprinkle with cheese and bake an additional 5 minutes or until cheese is melted and biscuits are golden. Let stand 5 minutes. Gently remove pizza cups from muffin pan and serve.

makes 10 pizza cups

prep time: 10 minutes
cook time: 25 minutes

take-along snack mix

1 tablespoon butter or
    margarine
2 tablespoons honey
1 cup toasted oat
    cereal, any flavor
½ cup coarsely broken
    pecans
½ cup thin pretzel sticks,
    broken in half
½ cup raisins
1 cup "M&M's"®
    Chocolate Mini
    Baking Bits

In large heavy skillet over low heat, melt butter; add honey and stir until blended. Add cereal, nuts, pretzels and raisins, stirring until all pieces are evenly coated. Continue cooking over low heat about 10 minutes, stirring frequently. Remove from heat; immediately spread on waxed paper until cool. Add "M&M's"® Chocolate Mini Baking Bits. Store in tightly covered container.

makes about 3½ cups

92

fantasy cinnamon applewiches

4 raisin bread slices

⅓ cup reduced-fat cream cheese

¼ cup finely chopped unpeeled apple

1 teaspoon sugar

⅛ teaspoon ground cinnamon

1. Toast bread. Cut into desired shapes using large cookie cutters.

2. Combine cream cheese and apple in small bowl; spread onto toast.

3. Combine sugar and cinnamon in another small bowl; sprinkle evenly over cream cheese mixture.

makes 4 servings

cook's tip: Get out the cookie cutters any time of the year for this fun treat. Or, create your own fun shapes—be sure to have an adult cut out the requested shapes with a serrated knife for best results.

savory cheddar bread

2 cups all-purpose flour

4 teaspoons baking powder

1 tablespoon sugar

½ teaspoon onion salt

½ teaspoon oregano, crushed

¼ teaspoon dry mustard

1 cup (4 ounces) SARGENTO® Fancy Mild or Sharp Cheddar Shredded Cheese

1 egg, beaten

1 cup milk

1 tablespoon butter or margarine, melted

In large bowl, stir together flour, baking powder, sugar, onion salt, oregano, dry mustard and cheese. In separate bowl, combine egg, milk and butter; add to dry ingredients, stirring just until moistened. Spread batter in greased 8×4-inch loaf pan. Bake at 350°F 45 minutes or until wooden pick inserted in center comes out clean. Cool 10 minutes on wire rack. Remove from pan.

makes 16 slices

94

ranch baked quesadillas

1 cup shredded cooked
    chicken

1 cup (4 ounces)
    shredded Monterey
    Jack cheese

½ cup HIDDEN VALLEY®
    Original Ranch®
    Dressing

¼ cup diced green
    chiles, rinsed and
    drained

4 (9-inch) flour tortillas,
    heated

    Salsa and guacamole
    (optional)

Combine chicken, cheese, dressing and chiles in a medium bowl. Place about ½ cup chicken mixture on each tortilla; fold in half. Place quesadillas on a baking sheet. Bake at 350°F. for 15 minutes or until cheese is melted. Cut into thirds, if desired. Serve with salsa and guacamole, if desired.

makes 4 servings

rocky road popcorn balls

6 cups unbuttered
    popped popcorn,
    lightly salted

2 cups "M&M's"®
    Chocolate Mini
    Baking Bits, divided

1¾ cups peanuts

¼ cup (½ stick) butter

4 cups miniature
    marshmallows,
    divided

In large bowl combine popcorn, 1½ cups "M&M's"® Chocolate Mini Baking Bits and peanuts; set aside. Place remaining ½ cup "M&M's"® Chocolate Mini Baking Bits in shallow bowl; set aside. In large saucepan over low heat, combine butter and marshmallows until melted, stirring often. Pour marshmallow mixture over popcorn mixture; stir until well coated. Form popcorn mixture into 12 balls; roll in "M&M's"® Chocolate Mini Baking Bits. Store in tightly covered container.

makes 12 popcorn balls

berry good dip

8 ounces fresh or thawed frozen strawberries

4 ounces cream cheese, softened

¼ cup reduced-fat sour cream

1 tablespoon sugar

1. Place strawberries in food processor or blender container; process until smooth.

2. Beat cream cheese in small bowl until smooth. Stir in sour cream, strawberry purée and sugar; cover. Refrigerate until ready to serve.

3. Spoon dip into small serving bowl. Garnish with orange peel, if desired. Serve with assorted fresh fruit dippers or angel food cake cubes.

makes 6 (¼-cup) servings

tip: For a super-quick fruit spread for toasted mini English muffins or bagels, beat 1 package (8 ounces) softened cream cheese in small bowl until fluffy. Stir in 3 to 4 tablespoons strawberry spreadable fruit. Season to taste with 1 to 2 teaspoons sugar, if desired. Makes 6 servings.

quick s'mores

1 whole graham cracker

1 large marshmallow

1 teaspoon hot fudge sauce

1. Break graham cracker in half crosswise. Place one half on small paper plate or microwavable plate; top with marshmallow.

2. Spread remaining ½ of cracker with fudge sauce.

3. Place cracker with marshmallow in microwave. Microwave at HIGH 12 to 14 seconds or until marshmallow puffs up. Immediately place remaining cracker, fudge side down, over marshmallow. Press crackers gently to even out marshmallow layer. Cool completely.

makes 1 serving

tip: S'mores can be made the night before and wrapped in plastic wrap or sealed in a small plastic food storage bag. Store at room temperature until ready to pack in your child's lunch box the next morning.

98

sweet treat tortillas

4 (7- to 8-inch) flour tortillas

4 ounces reduced-fat cream cheese, softened

¼ cup strawberry or other flavor spreadable fruit or preserves

1 medium banana, peeled and chopped

1. Spread each tortilla with 1 ounce cream cheese and 1 tablespoon spreadable fruit; top with ¼ of the banana.

2. Roll up tortillas; cut crosswise into thirds.   *makes 6 servings*

more sweet treats: Substitute your favorite chopped fruit for banana.

cinnamon-spice treats: Omit spreadable fruit and banana. Mix small amounts of sugar, ground cinnamon and nutmeg into cream cheese; spread evenly onto tortillas. Sprinkle lightly with desired amount of chopped pecans or walnuts. Top with chopped fruit, if desired; roll up. Cut crosswise into thirds.

señor nacho dip

4 ounces reduced-fat cream cheese

½ cup (2 ounces) reduced-fat Cheddar cheese

¼ cup mild or medium chunky salsa

2 teaspoons low-fat (2%) milk

4 ounces baked tortilla chips or assorted fresh vegetable dippers

1. Combine cream cheese and Cheddar cheese in small saucepan; stir over low heat until melted. Stir in salsa and milk; heat thoroughly, stirring occasionally.

2. Transfer dip to small serving bowl. Serve with tortilla chips. Garnish with hot peppers and cilantro, if desired.   *makes 4 servings*

olé dip: Substitute reduced-fat Monterey Jack cheese or taco cheese for Cheddar cheese.

spicy mustard dip: Omit tortilla chips. Substitute 2 teaspoons spicy brown or honey mustard for salsa. Serve with fresh vegetable dippers or pretzels.

brontosaurus bites

4 cups air-popped
popcorn

2 cups mini-dinosaur
grahams

2 cups corn cereal
squares

1½ cups dried pineapple
wedges

1 package (6 ounces)
dried fruit bits

Butter-flavored
nonstick cooking
spray

1 tablespoon plus
1½ teaspoons sugar

1½ teaspoons ground
cinnamon

½ teaspoon ground
nutmeg

1 cup yogurt-covered
raisins

1. Preheat oven to 350°F. Combine popcorn, grahams, cereal, pineapple and fruit bits in large bowl; mix lightly. Transfer to 15×10-inch jelly-roll pan. Spray mixture generously with cooking spray.

2. Combine sugar, cinnamon and nutmeg in small bowl. Sprinkle ½ of sugar mixture over popcorn mixture; toss lightly to coat. Spray mixture again with additional cooking spray. Add remaining sugar mixture; mix lightly.

3. Bake snack mix 10 minutes, stirring after 5 minutes. Cool completely in pan on wire rack. Add raisins; mix lightly.

makes 12 (¾-cup) servings

gorilla grub: Substitute plain raisins for the yogurt-covered raisins and ¼ cup grated Parmesan cheese for the sugar, cinnamon and nutmeg.

tip: For individual party take-home treats, wrap snack mix in festive colored paper napkins.

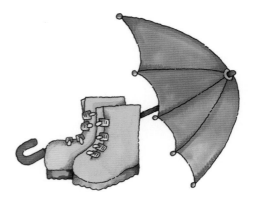

pizza turnovers

5 ounces reduced-fat Italian bulk turkey sausage (mild)

½ cup pizza sauce

Nonstick olive oil cooking spray

1 (10-ounce) package refrigerated pizza dough

⅓ cup shredded reduced-fat Italian blend cheese

1. Preheat oven to 425°F. Cook sausage in nonstick saucepan until browned, stirring with spoon to break up meat. Drain off fat. Stir in pizza sauce. Cook until hot.

2. Spray baking sheet with cooking spray. Unroll pizza dough onto baking sheet. Pat into 12×8-inch rectangle. Cut into six (4×4-inch) squares. Divide sausage mixture evenly among squares. Sprinkle with cheese. Lift one corner of each square and fold dough over filling to opposite corner, making a triangle. Press edges with tines of fork to seal.

3. Bake 11 to 13 minutes or until golden brown. Serve immediately or follow directions for freezing and reheating. *makes 6 servings*

note: To freeze turnovers, remove to wire rack to cool for 30 minutes. Individually wrap in plastic wrap, place in freezer container or plastic freezer bag and freeze. To reheat turnovers, preheat oven to 400°F. Unwrap turnovers. Place on ungreased baking pan. Cover loosely with foil. Bake for 18 to 22 minutes or until hot. Or, place one turnover on a paper-towel-lined microwavable plate. Heat on DEFROST (30% power) 3 to 3½ minutes or until hot, turning once.

painted bread knots

1 tablespoon *French's*® Classic Yellow® Mustard

1 tablespoon milk

1 container (11 ounces) refrigerated crusty French loaf dough

Coarse salt

1. Preheat oven to 350°F. Combine mustard and milk in small bowl. Cut bread dough into 12 (1-inch) slices. Roll each slice into 8-inch long piece. Tie each into knot.

2. Arrange knots on lightly greased baking sheet. Paint each with mustard mixture. Sprinkle with salt. Bake 20 minutes or until golden. Transfer baking sheet to wire rack and let knots stand on baking sheet until completely cool.

3. Serve with additional mustard. *makes 12 servings*

prep time: 10 minutes
cook time: 20 minutes

original ranch® & cheddar bread

1 cup HIDDEN VALLEY® Original Ranch® Dressing

2 cups (8 ounces) shredded sharp Cheddar cheese

1 whole loaf (1 pound) French bread (not sour dough)

Stir together dressing and cheese. Cut bread in half lengthwise. Place on a broiler pan and spread dressing mixture evenly over cut side of each half. Broil until lightly brown. Cut each half into 8 pieces.

makes 16 pieces

no-bake banana peanut butter fudge bars

1 ripe, large DOLE® Banana

⅔ cup butter or margarine

2 teaspoons vanilla extract

2½ cups rolled oats

½ cup packed brown sugar

1 cup semisweet chocolate chips

½ cup peanut butter

• Finely chop banana (1¼ cups). Melt butter in large skillet over medium heat; stir in vanilla. Add oats and brown sugar. Heat and stir 5 minutes. Set aside ¾ cup oat mixture. Press remaining oat mixture into greased 9-inch square baking pan. Sprinkle banana over crust.

• Melt chocolate chips and peanut butter together over low heat. Pour and spread over banana. Sprinkle with reserved oat mixture; press down lightly. Chill 2 hours before cutting. Store in refrigerator.

makes 24 bars

106

quick pizza snacks

3 English muffins, split
   and toasted

1 can (14½ ounces)
   Italian-style diced
   tomatoes, undrained

¾ cup (3 ounces)
   shredded Italian
   cheese blend

   Bell pepper strips
   (optional)

Preheat oven to 350°F. Place English muffin halves on ungreased baking sheet. Top each muffin with ¼ cup tomatoes; sprinkle with 2 tablespoons cheese. Bake about 5 minutes or until cheese is melted and lightly browned. Top with pepper strips, if desired.

makes 6 servings

inside-out turkey sandwiches

2 tablespoons cream
   cheese

2 tablespoons
   pasteurized process
   cheese spread

2 teaspoons chopped
   green onion tops

1 teaspoon prepared
   mustard

12 thin round slices
   turkey breast
   or smoked turkey
   breast

4 large pretzel logs or
   unsalted bread
   sticks

1. Combine cream cheese, process cheese spread, green onion and mustard in small bowl; mix well.

2. Arrange 3 turkey slices on large sheet of plastic wrap, overlapping slices in center. Spread ¼ of cheese mixture evenly onto turkey slices, covering slices completely. Place 1 pretzel at bottom edge of turkey slices; roll up turkey around pretzel. (Be sure to keep all 3 turkey slices together as you roll them around pretzel.)

3. Repeat with remaining ingredients.

makes 4 servings

pleasin' peanutty snack mix

4 cups whole wheat
   cereal squares *or*
   2 cups whole wheat
   and 2 cups corn or
   rice cereal squares

2 cups small pretzel
   twists or goldfish-
   shaped pretzels

½ cup dry-roasted
   peanuts

2 tablespoons creamy
   peanut butter

1 tablespoon honey

1 tablespoon apple juice
   or water

2 teaspoons vanilla

   Vegetable oil or
   butter-flavored
   nonstick cooking
   spray

½ cup raisins, dried fruit
   bits or dried
   cherries (optional)

1. Preheat oven to 250°F.

2. Combine cereal, pretzels and peanuts in large bowl; set aside.

3. Combine peanut butter, honey and apple juice in 1-cup glass measure or small microwavable bowl. Microwave at HIGH 30 seconds or until hot. Stir in vanilla.

4. Drizzle peanut butter mixture evenly over cereal mixture; toss lightly to evenly coat. Place mixture in single layer in ungreased 15×10-inch jelly-roll pan; coat lightly with cooking spray.

5. Bake 8 minutes; stir. Continue baking 8 to 9 minutes or until golden brown. Remove from oven. Add raisins, if desired; mix lightly.

6. Spread mixture in single layer on large sheet of foil to cool.

makes 10 (⅔-cup) servings

Snack mixes are the perfect take-along food—just package them in small resealable plastic food storage bags and they're ready to go to any after-school activities or extra-long car trips. And, you can customize any snack mix to your child's tastes: substitute his or her favorite cereal and fruit to make the treat a special one.

110

swimming tuna dip

**1 cup low-fat (1%)
cottage cheese**

**1 tablespoon reduced-
fat mayonnaise**

**1 tablespoon lemon
juice**

**2 teaspoons dry ranch-
style salad dressing
mix**

**1 can (3 ounces) chunk
white tuna packed
in water, drained
and flaked**

**2 tablespoons sliced
green onion or
chopped celery**

**1 teaspoon dried
parsley flakes**

**1 package (12 ounces)
peeled baby carrots**

Combine cottage cheese, mayonnaise, lemon juice and salad dressing mix in food processor or blender. Cover and blend until smooth. Stir in tuna, green onion and parsley. Serve with carrots.

makes 4 servings

make your own pizza shapes

1 package (10 ounces) refrigerated pizza dough

¼ to ½ cup prepared pizza sauce

1 cup shredded mozzarella cheese

1 cup *French's*® *Taste Toppers*™ French Fried Onions

1. Preheat oven to 425°F. Unroll dough onto greased baking sheet. Press or roll dough into 12×8-inch rectangle. With sharp knife or pizza cutter, cut dough into large shape of your choice (butterfly, heart, star). Reroll scraps and cut into mini shapes. (See tip.)

2. Pre-bake crust 7 minutes or until crust just begins to brown. Spread with sauce and top with cheese. Bake 6 minutes or until crust is deep golden brown.

3. Sprinkle with *Taste Toppers*. Bake 2 minutes longer or until golden.

makes 4 to 6 servings

tip: Pizza dough can be cut with 6-inch shaped cookie cutters. Spread with sauce and top with cheese. Bake about 10 minutes or until crust is golden. Sprinkle with *Taste Toppers*. Bake 2 minutes longer.

prep time: 10 minutes
cook time: 15 minutes

peanut butter spread

2 tablespoons peanut butter

½ cup part skim ricotta cheese

1 tablespoon brown sugar

¼ teaspoon cinnamon

4 flour tortillas

1 sliced banana or apple, or jam

Mix peanut butter, ricotta cheese, brown sugar and cinnamon together. Spread over tortillas and with banana, apple or jam. Roll up tortillas. Keep extra spread refrigerated.

makes 4 servings

Favorite recipe from **The Sugar Association, Inc.**

soft pretzels

- 1 package (16 ounces) hot roll mix plus ingredients to prepare mix
- 1 egg white
- 2 teaspoons water
- 2 tablespoons *each* assorted coatings: grated Parmesan cheese, sesame seeds, poppy seeds, dried oregano leaves

1. Prepare hot roll mix according to package directions.

2. Preheat oven to 375°F. Spray baking sheets with nonstick cooking spray; set aside.

3. Divide dough equally into 16 pieces; roll each piece with hands to form a rope, 7 to 10 inches long. Place on prepared cookie sheets; form into desired shape (hearts, wreaths, pretzels, snails, loops, etc.).

4. Beat together egg white and water in small bowl until foamy. Brush onto dough shapes; sprinkle each shape with 1½ teaspoons of one of the coatings.

5. Bake until golden brown, about 15 minutes. Serve warm or at room temperature. *makes 16 pretzels*

fruit twists: Omit coatings. Prepare dough and roll into ropes as directed. Place ropes on lightly floured surface. Roll out, or pat, each rope into rectangle, ¼ inch thick; brush each rectangle with about 1 teaspoon spreadable fruit or preserves. Fold each rectangle lengthwise in half; twist into desired shape. Bake as directed.

cheese twists: Omit coatings. Prepare dough and roll into ropes as directed. Place ropes on lightly floured surface. Roll out, or pat, each rope into rectangle, ¼ inch thick. Sprinkle each rectangle with about 1 tablespoon shredded Cheddar or other cheese. Fold each rectangle lengthwise in half; twist into desired shape. Bake as directed.

taco popcorn olé

9 cups air-popped popcorn

Butter-flavored cooking spray

1 teaspoon chili powder

½ teaspoon salt

½ teaspoon garlic powder

⅛ teaspoon ground red pepper (optional)

1. Preheat oven to 350°F. Line 15×10-inch jelly-roll pan with foil.

2. Place popcorn in single layer in prepared pan. Coat lightly with cooking spray.

3. Combine chili powder, salt, garlic powder and red pepper, if desired, in small bowl; sprinkle over popcorn. Mix lightly to coat evenly.

4. Bake 5 minutes or until hot, stirring gently after 3 minutes. Spread mixture in single layer on large sheet of foil to cool.

makes 6 (1½-cup) servings

cook's tip: Store popcorn mixture in tightly covered container at room temperature up to 4 days.

original ranch® snack mix

8 cups Kellogg's® Crispix®* cereal

2½ cups small pretzels

2½ cups bite-size Cheddar cheese crackers (optional)

3 tablespoons vegetable oil

1 packet (1 ounce) HIDDEN VALLEY® Original Ranch® Salad Dressing & Recipe Mix

*Kellogg's® and Crispix® are registered trademarks of Kellogg Company.

Combine cereal, pretzels and crackers in a gallon-size Glad® Zipper Storage Bag. Pour oil over mixture. Seal bag and toss to coat. Add salad dressing & recipe mix; seal bag and toss again until coated.

makes 10 cups

summer fruits with peanut butter-honey dip

SNACKS

⅓ cup smooth or chunky peanut butter

2 tablespoons milk

2 tablespoons honey

1 tablespoon apple juice or water

⅛ teaspoon ground cinnamon

2 cups melon balls, including cantaloupe and honeydew

1 peach or nectarine, pitted and cut into 8 wedges

1 banana, peeled and thickly sliced

1. Place peanut butter in small bowl; gradually stir in milk and honey until blended. Stir in apple juice and cinnamon until mixture is smooth.

2. Serve dip with prepared fruits.

makes 4 servings (about ½ cup dip)

go-with suggestions: Serve after a spicy Thai or Asian dinner.

prep time: 20 minutes

banana s'mores

1 firm DOLE® Banana, sliced

12 graham cracker squares

6 large marshmallows

1 bar (1.55 ounces) milk chocolate candy

MICROWAVE DIRECTIONS

• Arrange 4 banana slices on each of 6 graham cracker squares. Top with marshmallow. Microwave on HIGH 12 to 15 seconds or until puffed.

• Place 2 squares chocolate on remaining 6 graham crackers. Microwave on HIGH 1 minute or until just soft. Put halves together to make sandwiches.

makes 6 servings

prep time: 5 minutes
cook time: 1 minute

118

DINNER

octo-dogs and shells

4 hot dogs

1½ cups uncooked small shell pasta

1½ cups frozen mixed vegetables

1 cup prepared Alfredo sauce

Prepared yellow mustard in squeeze bottle

Cheese-flavored fish-shaped crackers

Lay 1 hot dog on side with end facing you. Starting 1 inch from one end of hot dog, slice hot dog vertically in half. Roll hot dog ¼ turn and slice in half vertically again, making 4 segments connected at the top. Slice each segment in half vertically, creating a total of 8 "legs." Repeat with remaining hot dogs.

Place hot dogs in medium saucepan; cover with water. Bring to a boil over medium-high heat. Remove from heat; set aside.

Prepare pasta according to package directions, stirring in vegetables during last 3 minutes of cooking time. Drain; return to pan. Stir in Alfredo sauce. Heat over low heat until heated through. Divide pasta mixture between four plates.

Drain octo-dogs. Arrange one octo-dog on top of pasta mixture on each plate. Draw faces on "heads" of octo-dogs with mustard. Sprinkle crackers over pasta mixture.

makes 4 servings

ragú® pizza burgers

1 pound ground beef

2 cups RAGÚ® Old World Style® Pasta Sauce

1 cup shredded mozzarella cheese (about 4 ounces)

¼ teaspoon salt

6 English muffins, split and toasted

1. In small bowl, combine ground beef, ½ cup Ragú Pasta Sauce, ½ cup cheese and salt. Shape into 6 patties. Grill or broil until done.

2. Meanwhile, heat remaining pasta sauce. To serve, arrange burgers on muffin halves. Top with remaining cheese, sauce and muffin halves.

makes 6 servings

prep time: 10 minutes
cook time: 15 minutes

school night chicken rice taco toss

1 (6.9-ounce) package RICE-A-RONI® Chicken Flavor

2 tablespoons margarine or butter

1 (16-ounce) jar salsa

1 pound boneless, skinless chicken breasts, chopped

1 cup frozen or canned corn, drained

4 cups shredded lettuce

½ cup (2 ounces) shredded Cheddar cheese

2 cups tortilla chips, coarsely broken

1 medium tomato, chopped

1. In large skillet over medium-high heat, sauté rice-vermicelli mix with margarine until vermicelli is golden brown.

2. Slowly stir in 2 cups water, salsa, chicken and Special Seasonings. Bring to a boil. Reduce heat to low. Cover; simmer 10 minutes.

3. Stir in corn. Cover; simmer 5 to 10 minutes or until rice is tender and chicken is no longer pink inside.

4. Arrange lettuce on large serving platter. Top with chicken-rice mixture. Sprinkle with cheese and tortilla chips. Garnish with tomato.

makes 6 servings

prep time: 10 minutes
cook time: 30 minutes

123

crunchy fish sticks with rainbow parmesan pasta

⅔ cup milk

2 tablespoons margarine or butter

1 (5.1-ounce) package PASTA RONI® Angel Hair Pasta with Parmesan Cheese

2 cups frozen mixed vegetables or frozen chopped broccoli

Crunchy Fish Sticks (recipe follows)

1. In large saucepan, bring 1⅓ cups water, milk and margarine to a boil.

2. Stir in pasta, vegetables and Special Seasonings; bring back to a boil. Reduce heat to medium. Gently boil uncovered, 4 to 5 minutes or until pasta is tender. Let stand 3 minutes before serving. Serve with Crunchy Fish Sticks or prepared frozen fish sticks.

makes 4 servings

prep time: 20 minutes
cook time: 15 minutes

crunchy fish sticks

3 tablespoons all-purpose flour

½ teaspoon ground black pepper

1 large egg

2 tablespoons milk

3 cups cornflakes, coarsely crushed

1 pound cod fillets, cut into 3×1-inch strips and patted dry

½ to ¾ cup vegetable oil

1. In shallow bowl, combine flour and pepper; set aside. In small bowl, combine egg and milk; set aside. In another shallow bowl, place crushed cornflakes; set aside.

2. Coat fish in flour mixture, dip in egg mixture, then roll in cornflakes, pressing coating gently on each fish strip.

3. In large skillet over medium heat, heat oil. Add fish strips; cook 3 to 4 minutes on each side or until golden brown and fish is cooked through. Drain.

makes 4 servings

quick & easy chili

- **1 pound ground beef**
- **1 cup (1 small) chopped onion**
- **2 cloves garlic, finely chopped**
- **3½ cups (two 15-ounce cans) kidney, pinto or black beans, drained**
- **2½ cups (24-ounce jar) ORTEGA® Thick & Chunky Salsa, hot, medium or mild**
- **½ cup (4-ounce can) ORTEGA® Diced Green Chiles**
- **2 teaspoons chili powder**
- **½ teaspoon dried oregano, crushed**
- **½ teaspoon ground cumin**
- **Topping suggestions: ORTEGA® Thick and Chunky Salsa, shredded Cheddar cheese or Monterey Jack cheese, chopped tomatoes, sliced ripe olives, sliced green onions and sour cream**

COOK beef, onion and garlic in large skillet over medium-high heat for 4 to 5 minutes or until beef is no longer pink; drain.

STIR in beans, salsa, chiles, chili powder, oregano and cumin. Bring to a boil. Reduce heat to low; cook, covered, for 20 to 25 minutes.

TOP as desired before serving.   *makes 6 servings*

Why not spend just a few extra minutes in the kitchen and make a double or triple batch of chili? Chili freezes extremely well, and it's always helpful to have a few dinners ready to go at a moment's notice. You can freeze the chili in family-size portions, or freeze it in individual servings in resealable plastic freezer bags—that way the kids can grab a bag and reheat it in the microwave whenever they need to.

cheesy broccoli

2 tablespoons CRISCO® Oil*

2 cups broccoli flowerets

3 tablespoons water

½ teaspoon salt

¼ cup freshly grated Parmesan cheese

Use your favorite Crisco Oil product.

1. Heat oil in wok or large skillet on medium-high heat. Add broccoli. Cook and stir 2 minutes.

2. Add water and salt. Cover pan. Steam 3 minutes. Remove broccoli from pan with slotted spoon. Toss with cheese. Serve immediately.

makes 4 servings

prep time: 5 minutes
total time: 10 minutes

spicy chicken stromboli

1 cup frozen broccoli florets, thawed

1 can (10 ounces) diced chicken

1½ cups (6 ounces) shredded Monterey Jack cheese with jalapeño peppers

¼ cup chunky salsa

2 green onions, chopped

1 can (10 ounces) refrigerated pizza dough

1. Preheat oven to 400°F. Coarsely chop broccoli. Combine broccoli, chicken, cheese, salsa and green onions in small bowl.

2. Unroll pizza dough. Pat into 15×10-inch rectangle. Sprinkle broccoli mixture evenly over top. Starting with long side, tightly roll into log jelly-roll style. Pinch seam to seal. Place on baking sheet, seam side down.

3. Bake 15 to 20 minutes or until golden brown. Transfer to wire rack to cool slightly. Slice and serve warm.

makes 6 servings

serving suggestion: Serve with salsa on the side for dipping or pour salsa on top of slices for a boost of added flavor.

prep and cook time: 30 minutes

ham & cheese shells & trees

**2 tablespoons
margarine or butter**

**1 (6.2-ounce) package
PASTA RONI® Shells
& White Cheddar**

**2 cups fresh or frozen
chopped broccoli**

⅔ cup milk

**1½ cups ham or cooked
turkey, cut into thin
strips (about
6 ounces)**

1. In large saucepan, bring 2 cups water and margarine to a boil.

2. Stir in pasta. Reduce heat to medium. Gently boil uncovered,
6 minutes, stirring occasionally. Stir in broccoli; return to a boil. Boil
6 to 8 minutes or until most of water is absorbed.

3. Stir in milk, ham and Special Seasonings. Return to a boil; boil 1 to
2 minutes or until pasta is tender. Let stand 5 minutes before serving.

makes 4 servings

tip: No leftovers? Ask the deli to slice a ½-inch-thick piece of ham or
turkey.

prep time: 5 minutes
cook time: 20 minutes

tuna skillet supper

**1 package (8 ounces)
cream cheese,
softened**

1 cup milk

**1 packet (1 ounce)
HIDDEN VALLEY®
Original Ranch®
Salad Dressing &
Recipe Mix**

**8 ounces uncooked
spiral egg noodles**

**2 cups frozen petite
peas, thawed**

**2 cans (6 ounces each)
tuna or shrimp,
drained**

In a food processor fitted with a metal blade, blend cream cheese, milk
and salad dressing & recipe mix until smooth.

Cook pasta according to package directions; drain and combine with
peas and tuna in a large skillet. Stir dressing mixture into pasta. Cook
over low heat until mixture is hot. *makes 4 to 6 servings*

campfire hot dogs

½ **pound ground beef**

2 **cups RAGÚ® Old World Style® Pasta Sauce**

1 **can (10¾ to 16 ounces) baked beans**

8 **frankfurters, cooked**

8 **frankfurter rolls**

1. In 12-inch skillet, brown ground beef over medium-high heat; drain.

2. Stir in Ragú Pasta Sauce and beans. Bring to a boil over high heat. Reduce heat to low and simmer, stirring occasionally, 5 minutes.

3. To serve, arrange frankfurters in rolls and top with sauce mixture. Garnish, if desired, with Cheddar cheese. *makes 8 servings*

tip: For Chili Campfire Hot Dogs, simply stir 2 to 3 teaspoons chili powder into sauce mixture.

prep time: 5 minutes
cook time: 10 minutes

cheddar burger mashed potato bake

2 **pounds ground beef**

1 **medium onion, chopped**

1 **jar (16 ounces) RAGÚ® Cheese Creations!® Double Cheddar Sauce**

2 **teaspoons dry mustard**

4 **cups prepared mashed potatoes**

Preheat oven to 425°F. In 12-inch skillet, brown ground beef over medium-high heat; drain. Add onion and cook, stirring occasionally, 2 minutes. Stir in Ragú Cheese Creations! Sauce, mustard and, if desired, salt and ground black pepper to taste. Simmer uncovered, stirring occasionally, 3 minutes or until heated through.

Turn into 2-quart casserole; evenly top with mashed potatoes. Bake 25 minutes or until potatoes are lightly golden. *makes 8 servings*

recipe tip: When making mashed potatoes, use Idaho or all-purpose potatoes for marvelous flavor and texture. Heat the milk before adding it—this minimizes any starchiness.

macaroni & cheese boats

1 box (7.25 ounces)
    macaroni & cheese
    mix
¼ cup milk
¼ cup butter
1½ cups shredded
    Cheddar cheese,
    divided
1 tablespoon *French's®*
    Worcestershire
    Sauce
4 red, green or yellow
    bell peppers, halved
    lengthwise
1⅓ cups *French's® Taste
    Toppers™* French
    Fried Onions

1. In medium saucepan, prepare macaroni & cheese as directed on package using ¼ cup milk and ¼ cup butter. Stir in *1 cup* cheese and Worcestershire; set aside.

2. Arrange peppers cut side up in glass baking dish. Add *¼ cup water* to baking dish and cover. Microwave on HIGH 5 minutes or until crisp-tender; drain.

3. Spoon macaroni & cheese into peppers and sprinkle with remaining cheese. Sprinkle with **Taste Toppers** and microwave 2 minutes.

makes 4 servings

prep time: 10 minutes
cook time: 7 minutes

veggie ravioli

2 cans (15 ounces each)
    ravioli
1 bag (16 ounces)
    BIRDS EYE® frozen
    Mixed Vegetables
2 cups shredded
    mozzarella cheese

• In 1½-quart microwave-safe casserole dish, combine ravioli and vegetables.

• Cover; microwave on HIGH 10 minutes, stirring halfway through cook time.

• Uncover; sprinkle with cheese. Microwave 5 minutes more or until cheese is melted.

makes 6 servings

serving suggestion: Sprinkle with grated Parmesan cheese.

prep time: 5 minutes
cook time: 15 minutes

132

ravioli stew

- 1 tablespoon olive or vegetable oil
- 3 medium carrots, chopped
- 2 medium ribs celery, chopped
- 1 onion, chopped
- 1 jar (26 to 28 ounces) RAGÚ® Hearty Robusto!™ Pasta Sauce
- 1 can (14½ ounces) chicken broth
- 1 cup water
- 1 package (12 to 16 ounces) fresh or frozen mini ravioli, cooked and drained

1. In 6-quart saucepot, heat oil over medium-high heat and cook carrots, celery and onion, stirring occasionally, 8 minutes or until golden.

2. Stir in Ragú Pasta Sauce, broth and water. Bring to a boil over high heat. Reduce heat to low and simmer covered 15 minutes.

3. Just before serving, stir in hot ravioli and season, if desired, with salt and ground black pepper. Garnish, if desired, with fresh basil.

makes 6 servings

prep time: 10 minutes
cook time: 30 minutes

barbecued meat loaf

- 1 envelope LIPTON® RECIPE SECRETS® Onion Soup Mix
- 2 pounds ground beef
- 1½ cups fresh bread crumbs
- 2 eggs
- ¾ cup water
- ⅔ cup barbecue sauce

1. Preheat oven to 350°F. In large bowl, combine all ingredients except ⅓ cup barbecue sauce.

2. In 13×9-inch baking or roasting pan, shape beef mixture into loaf. Top with reserved barbecue sauce.

3. Bake, uncovered, 1 hour or until done. Let stand 10 minutes before serving.

makes 8 servings

134

sausage cheeseburger pizza

1 pound BOB EVANS® Original Recipe Roll Sausage

1 (12-inch) prepared pizza shell

½ cup yellow mustard

2 cups (8 ounces) shredded mozzarella cheese

½ cup chopped onion

15 dill pickle slices

¾ cup (3 ounces) shredded Cheddar cheese

Preheat oven to 425°F. Crumble and cook sausage in medium skillet until browned; drain well on paper towels. Place pizza dough on lightly greased 12-inch pizza pan or baking sheet. Spread mustard over pizza shell; top with mozzarella cheese, sausage and onion. Place pickle slices evenly on top; sprinkle with Cheddar cheese. Bake 12 minutes or until shell is cooked through and cheese is bubbly. Cut into thin wedges or squares and serve hot. Refrigerate leftovers.

makes about 10 appetizer servings

sloppy dogs

1 can (15 ounces) pinto or kidney beans, drained

1 can (14½ ounces) DEL MONTE® Zesty Chili Style Chunky Tomatoes

2 fully cooked hot dogs, sliced crosswise

1 teaspoon prepared mustard

4 hamburger buns, split

½ cup shredded Cheddar cheese

MICROWAVE DIRECTIONS

1. Combine all ingredients, except buns and cheese, in 2-quart microwavable dish. Cover and microwave on HIGH 6 to 8 minutes or until heated through.

2. Place buns on paper towel; microwave on HIGH 30 seconds to 1 minute. Place buns on 4 dishes, cut side up.

3. Spoon chili over buns. Top with cheese. Serve immediately.

makes 4 servings

prep time: 5 minutes
cook time: 9 minutes

barbecue chicken with cornbread topper

DINNER

1½ pounds boneless skinless chicken breasts and thighs

1 can (15 ounces) red beans, drained and rinsed

1 can (8 ounces) tomato sauce

1 cup chopped green bell pepper

½ cup barbecue sauce

1 envelope (6.5 ounces) cornbread mix

Ingredients for cornbread mix

1. Cut chicken into ¾-inch cubes. Heat nonstick skillet over medium heat. Add chicken; cook and stir 5 minutes or until cooked through.

2. Combine chicken, beans, tomato sauce, bell pepper and barbecue sauce in 8-inch microwavable ovenproof dish.

3. Preheat oven to 375°F. Loosely cover chicken mixture with plastic wrap or waxed paper. Microwave on MEDIUM-HIGH (70% power) 8 minutes or until heated through, stirring after 4 minutes.

4. While chicken mixture is heating, prepare cornbread mix according to package directions. Spoon batter over chicken mixture. Bake 15 to 18 minutes or until toothpick inserted in center of cornbread layer comes out clean.

makes 8 servings

sweet potato apple bake

3 cups mashed sweet potatoes

2 to 3 medium apples, peeled, sliced

Ground cinnamon

½ cup apple jelly

Preheat oven to 350°F. Spray 9-inch glass pie plate with nonstick cooking spray. Fill dish evenly with mashed sweet potatoes. Arrange apple slices on top. Sprinkle apples with cinnamon. Melt apple jelly over low heat in small saucepan. Brush over apples. Bake 30 minutes or until apples are tender.

makes 6 side-dish servings

Favorite recipe from **New York Apple Association, Inc.**

oven "fried" chicken

2 (4-ounce) boneless skinless chicken breasts, cut in half

4 small (2½ ounces each) skinless chicken drumsticks

1½ cups cornflakes, crushed

1 tablespoon dried parsley flakes

3 tablespoons all-purpose flour

½ teaspoon poultry seasoning

¼ teaspoon garlic salt

¼ teaspoon black pepper

1 egg white

1 tablespoon water

Nonstick cooking spray

1. Preheat oven to 375°F. Rinse chicken. Trim off any fat. Pat dry with paper towels.

2. Mix together cornflake crumbs and parsley in shallow bowl. Combine flour, poultry seasoning, garlic salt and pepper in resealable plastic food storage bag. Whisk together egg white and water in small bowl.

3. Add chicken to flour mixture, one or two pieces at a time. Seal bag; shake until chicken is well coated. Remove chicken from bag, shaking off excess flour. Dip into egg white mixture, coating all sides. Roll in crumb mixture. Place in shallow baking pan. Repeat with remaining chicken, flour mixture, egg white and crumb mixture.

4. Lightly spray chicken pieces with cooking spray. Bake breast pieces 18 to 20 minutes or until no longer pink in center. Bake drumsticks about 25 minutes or until juices run clear.   *makes 4 servings*

taco taters

1 pound ground beef

1 jar (26 to 28 ounces) RAGÚ® Old World Style® Pasta Sauce

1 package (1.25 ounces) taco seasoning mix

6 large all-purpose potatoes, unpeeled and baked

1. In 12-inch skillet, brown ground beef over medium-high heat; drain. Stir in Ragú Pasta Sauce and taco seasoning mix and cook 5 minutes.

2. To serve, cut a lengthwise slice from top of each potato. Evenly spoon beef mixture onto each potato. Garnish, if desired, with shredded Cheddar cheese and sour cream.   *makes 6 servings*

prep time: 5 minutes
cook time: 15 minutes

138

creamy mashed potato bake

3 cups mashed
    potatoes

1 cup sour cream

¼ cup milk

¼ teaspoon garlic
    powder

1⅓ cups *French's® Taste
    Toppers™* French
    Fried Onions,
    divided

1 cup (4 ounces)
    shredded Cheddar
    cheese, divided

1. Preheat oven to 350°F. Combine mashed potatoes, sour cream, milk and garlic powder.

2. Spoon half of mixture into 2-quart casserole. Sprinkle with ⅔ cup *Taste Toppers* and ½ cup cheese. Top with remaining potato mixture.

3. Bake 30 minutes or until hot. Top with remaining ⅔ cup *Taste Toppers* and ½ cup cheese. Bake 5 minutes or until *Taste Toppers* are golden.

makes 6 servings

prep time: 5 minutes
cook time: 35 minutes

philly cheese steak sandwich

1 onion, sliced

1 green bell pepper, cut
    into thin strips

2 tablespoons butter or
    margarine

2 packages (6 ounces
    each) HILLSHIRE
    FARM® Deli Select
    Roast Beef, cut into
    thin strips

4 submarine or hoagie
    rolls, cut into halves

½ pound provolone
    cheese, sliced

Sauté onion and bell pepper in butter in medium saucepan over medium-high heat until onion is transparent. Mix in Roast Beef; heat until beef is warm. Evenly divide beef mixture into 4 portions; fill each roll with beef mixture. Top each sandwich evenly with cheese.

makes 4 servings

140

hot dog macaroni

1 package (8 ounces) hot dogs

1 cup uncooked corkscrew pasta

1 cup shredded Cheddar cheese

1 box (10 ounces) BIRDS EYE® frozen Green Peas

1 cup 1% milk

- Slice hot dogs into bite-size pieces; set aside.

- In large saucepan, cook pasta according to package directions; drain and return to saucepan.

- Stir in hot dogs, cheese, peas and milk. Cook over medium heat 10 minutes or until cheese is melted, stirring occasionally.

makes 4 servings

prep time: 10 minutes
cook time: 20 minutes

pasta pronto

8 ounces linguine or spaghetti, uncooked

1 pound ground beef, ground turkey or mild Italian sausage

1 cup coarsely chopped onions

1 clove garlic, minced

2 cans (14½ ounces each) DEL MONTE® Pasta Style Chunky Tomatoes, undrained

1 can (8 ounces) DEL MONTE® Tomato Sauce

About ¼ cup (1 ounce) grated Parmesan cheese

1. Cook pasta according to package directions; drain and keep hot.

2. In large skillet, brown meat with onions and garlic; drain.

3. Add tomatoes and tomato sauce. Cook, stirring frequently, 15 minutes.

4. Spoon sauce over hot pasta; sprinkle with cheese. Serve with French bread, if desired. *makes 4 servings*

prep time: 10 minutes
cook time: 20 minutes

saucy chicken & vegetables

6 boneless skinless chicken breast halves

1 can (10¾ ounces) condensed cream of chicken soup

1⅓ cups *French's*® Taste Toppers™ French Fried Onions, divided

1 cup milk or water

½ cup grated Parmesan cheese

3 cups bite-size vegetables*

2 teaspoons dried basil leaves

*Try these variations: 3 cups cut-up tomatoes, zucchini and asparagus; 3 cups cut-up broccoli and carrots; 1 (16-ounce) package frozen vegetable combination, thawed.

1. Heat *1 tablespoon oil* in 12-inch nonstick skillet until hot. Cook chicken 10 minutes or until thoroughly browned on both sides. Remove; set aside.

2. In same skillet, combine soup, ⅔ cup *Taste Toppers*, milk and cheese. Heat to boiling. Stir in vegetables and basil. Return chicken to skillet. Reduce heat to medium-low. Cook 5 minutes or until chicken is no longer pink in center, stirring occasionally.

3. Top with remaining ⅔ cup *Taste Toppers*. Serve with hot cooked rice or pasta, if desired. *makes 6 servings*

tip: For a crispier onion topping, microwave *French's*® Taste Toppers™ 1 minute on HIGH.

prep time: 10 minutes
cook time: 20 minutes

corny sloppy joes

- **1 pound lean ground beef or ground turkey**
- **1 small onion, chopped**
- **1 can (15½ ounces) sloppy joe sauce**
- **1 box (10 ounces) BIRDS EYE® frozen Sweet Corn**
- **6 hamburger buns**

- In large skillet, cook beef and onion over high heat until beef is well browned.

- Stir in sloppy joe sauce and corn; reduce heat to low and simmer 5 minutes or until heated through.

- Serve mixture in hamburger buns.

makes 6 servings

serving suggestion: Sprinkle with shredded Cheddar cheese.

prep time: 5 minutes
cook time: 15 minutes

pizza casserole

- **1 pound BOB EVANS® Italian Roll Sausage**
- **12 ounces wide noodles, cooked according to package directions**
- **2 (14-ounce) jars pepperoni pizza sauce**
- **2 cups (8 ounces) shredded Cheddar cheese**
- **2 cups (8 ounces) shredded mozzarella cheese**
- **6 ounces sliced pepperoni**

Preheat oven to 350°F. Crumble and cook sausage in medium skillet over medium heat until browned. Drain on paper towels. Layer half of noodles in lightly greased 13×9-inch casserole dish. Top with half of sausage, half of pizza sauce, half of cheeses and half of pepperoni. Repeat layers with remaining ingredients, reserving several pepperoni slices for garnish on top of casserole. Bake 35 to 40 minutes. Refrigerate leftovers.

makes 6 to 8 servings

skillet franks and potatoes

3 tablespoons vegetable oil, divided

4 HEBREW NATIONAL® Quarter Pound Dinner Beef Franks or 4 Beef Knockwurst

3 cups chopped cooked red potatoes

1 cup chopped onion

1 cup chopped seeded green bell pepper or combination of green and red bell peppers

3 tablespoons chopped fresh parsley (optional)

1 teaspoon dried sage leaves

½ teaspoon salt

¼ teaspoon freshly ground black pepper

Heat 1 tablespoon oil in large nonstick skillet over medium heat. Score franks; add to skillet. Cook franks until browned. Transfer to plate; set aside.

Add remaining 2 tablespoons oil to skillet. Add potatoes, onion and bell pepper; cook and stir about 12 to 14 minutes or until potatoes are golden brown. Stir in parsley, sage, salt and pepper.

Return franks to skillet; push down into potato mixture. Cook about 5 minutes or until heated through, turning once halfway through cooking time.

makes 4 servings

Round red potatoes, also called boiling potatoes, have a waxy flesh; they contain more moisture and less starch than russet potatoes which makes them better suited for boiling. Leaving the peel on the potatoes adds extra flavor and nutrients (as well as color) to the dish; just scrub them well with a vegetable brush before cooking.

mini chicken pot pies

1 container (about 16 ounces) refrigerated reduced-fat buttermilk biscuits

1½ cups milk

1 package (1.8 ounces) white sauce mix

2 cups cut-up cooked chicken

1 cup frozen assorted vegetables, partially thawed

2 cups shredded Cheddar cheese

2 cups *French's® Taste Toppers™* French Fried Onions

1. Preheat oven to 400°F. Separate biscuits; press into 8 (8-ounce) custard cups, pressing up sides to form crust.

2. Whisk milk and sauce mix in medium saucepan. Bring to boiling over medium-high heat. Reduce heat to medium-low; simmer 1 minute, whisking constantly, until thickened. Stir in chicken and vegetables.

3. Spoon about ⅓ cup chicken mixture into each crust. Place cups on baking sheet. Bake 15 minutes or until golden brown. Top each with cheese and *Taste Toppers*. Bake 3 minutes or until golden. To serve, remove from cups and transfer to serving plates.   *makes 8 servings*

prep time: 15 minutes
cook time: about 20 minutes

groovy angel hair goulash

1 pound lean ground beef

2 tablespoons margarine or butter

1 (4.8-ounce) package PASTA RONI® Angel Hair Pasta with Herbs

1 (14½-ounce) can diced tomatoes, undrained

1 cup frozen or canned corn, drained

1. In large skillet over medium-high heat, brown ground beef. Remove from skillet; drain. Set aside.

2. In same skillet, bring 1½ cups water and margarine to a boil.

3. Stir in pasta; cook 1 minute or just until pasta softens slightly. Stir in tomatoes, corn, beef and Special Seasonings; return to a boil. Reduce heat to medium. Gently boil uncovered, 4 to 5 minutes or until pasta is tender, stirring frequently. Let stand 3 to 5 minutes before serving.

makes 4 servings

prep time: 5 minutes
cook time: 15 minutes

ranch crispy chicken

- ¼ **cup unseasoned dry bread crumbs or cornflake crumbs**
- 1 **packet (1 ounce) HIDDEN VALLEY® Original Ranch® Salad Dressing & Recipe Mix**
- 6 **bone-in chicken pieces**

Combine bread crumbs and salad dressing & recipe mix in a gallon-size Glad® Zipper Storage Bag. Add chicken pieces; seal bag. Shake to coat chicken. Bake chicken on ungreased baking pan at 375°F. for 50 minutes or until no longer pink in center and juices run clear.

makes 4 to 6 servings

ham and potato au gratin

- 3 **tablespoons butter or margarine**
- 3 **tablespoons all-purpose flour**
- 2 **cups milk**
- 1½ **cups (6 ounces) shredded Cheddar cheese**
- 1 **tablespoon Dijon mustard**
- 2 **cups HILLSHIRE FARM® Lean & Hearty Ham cut into thin strips**
- 1 **package (24 ounces) frozen shredded hash brown potatoes, thawed**
- 1 **package (10 ounces) frozen chopped spinach, thawed and drained**

Preheat oven to 350°F.

Melt butter in large saucepan over medium heat; stir in flour. Add milk. Cook and stir until bubbly; cook 1 minute more. Remove from heat. Stir in cheese and mustard; set aside.

Place ½ of Ham into ungreased medium casserole. Top ham with ½ of potatoes and ½ of milk mixture. Spoon spinach over top. Repeat layers with remaining ham, potatoes and milk mixture.

Bake, uncovered, 30 minutes or until heated through.

makes 8 servings

150

stuffed franks 'n' taters

4 cups frozen hash brown potatoes, thawed

1 can (10¾ ounces) condensed cream of celery soup

1⅓ cups *French's*® *Taste Toppers*™ French Fried Onions, divided

1 cup (4 ounces) shredded Cheddar cheese, divided

1 cup sour cream

½ teaspoon salt

¼ teaspoon pepper

6 frankfurters

Preheat oven to 400°F. In large bowl, combine potatoes, soup, ⅔ cup **Taste Toppers**, ½ cup cheese, sour cream and seasonings. Spread potato mixture in 12×8-inch baking dish. Split frankfurters lengthwise almost into halves. Arrange frankfurters, split-side up, along center of casserole. Bake, covered, at 400°F for 30 minutes or until heated through. Fill frankfurters with remaining cheese and ⅔ cup **Taste Toppers**; bake, uncovered, 1 to 3 minutes or until **Taste Toppers** are golden brown.
makes 6 servings

microwave directions: Prepare potato mixture as above; spread in 12×8-inch microwave-safe dish. Cook, covered, on HIGH 8 minutes; stir potato mixture halfway through cooking time. Split frankfurters and arrange on potatoes as above. Cook, covered, 4 to 6 minutes or until frankfurters are heated through. Rotate dish halfway through cooking time. Fill frankfurters with remaining cheese and ⅔ *cup* onions; cook, uncovered, 1 minute or until cheese melts. Let stand 5 minutes.

cinnamon apple rings

3 large cooking apples

¼ cup lemon juice

1 cup water

½ cup sugar

¼ cup red cinnamon candies

Peel and core apples; cut crosswise into ½-inch-thick rings. Toss with lemon juice to prevent discoloration. Combine water, sugar and candies in large saucepan. Bring to a boil, stirring until sugar and candies are dissolved. Add apple rings and simmer until just tender, about 15 minutes. Let cool in liquid. Drain.
makes 4 servings

Favorite recipe from **Perdue Farms Incorporated**

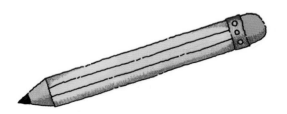

nifty nacho dinner

8 ounces lean ground beef

1 (6.8-ounce) package RICE-A-RONI® Beef Flavor

2 tablespoons margarine or butter

1 (16-ounce) can refried beans

1 (11-ounce) can Mexican-style corn or sweet corn, drained

1½ cups (6 ounces) shredded Cheddar cheese, divided

Tortilla chips

1. In large skillet over medium-high heat, brown ground beef. Remove from skillet; drain. Set aside.

2. In same skillet over medium heat, sauté rice-vermicelli mix with margarine until vermicelli is golden brown.

3. Slowly stir in 2½ cups water and Special Seasonings; bring to a boil. Reduce heat to low. Cover; simmer 10 minutes.

4. Stir in refried beans, corn, 1 cup cheese and beef; return to a simmer. Cover; simmer 5 to 10 minutes or until rice is tender. Top with remaining ½ cup cheese. Serve in skillet with tortilla chips.

makes 6 servings

prep time: 5 minutes
cook time: 30 minutes

taco cups

1 pound ground beef OR pork

1 package (1.0 ounce) LAWRY'S® Taco Spices & Seasonings

1¼ cups water

¼ cup mild salsa

2 packages (8 ounces each) refrigerator biscuits

½ cup (2 ounces) shredded cheddar cheese

In medium skillet, cook ground beef over medium-high heat until crumbly; drain fat. Add Taco Spices & Seasonings and water; mix well. Bring to a boil over medium-high heat; reduce heat to low and simmer, uncovered, 10 minutes. Stir in salsa. Separate biscuits and press each biscuit into an ungreased muffin cup. Spoon equal amounts of meat mixture into each muffin cup; sprinkle each with cheese. Bake, uncovered, in 350°F oven 12 minutes. *makes 12 pastries*

serving suggestion: Serve as a snack or a main dish.

hint: Flatten any leftover biscuit dough into disks; sprinkle with cinnamon-sugar mixture and bake in 350°F oven until golden.

kid's choice meatballs

- 1½ **pounds ground beef**
- ¼ **cup dry seasoned bread crumbs**
- ¼ **cup grated Parmesan cheese**
- 3 **tablespoons** *French's*® **Worcestershire Sauce**
- 1 **egg**
- 2 **jars (14 ounces** *each***) spaghetti sauce**

1. Preheat oven to 425°F. In bowl, gently mix beef, bread crumbs, cheese, Worcestershire and egg. Shape into 1-inch meatballs. Place on rack in roasting pan. Bake 15 minutes or until cooked.

2. In large saucepan, combine meatballs and spaghetti sauce. Cook until heated through. Serve over cooked pasta.

makes 6 to 8 servings (about 48 meatballs)

quick meatball tip: On waxed paper, pat meat mixture into 8×6×1-inch rectangle. With knife, cut crosswise and lengthwise into 1-inch rows. Roll each small square into a ball.

prep time: 10 minutes
cook time: 20 minutes

bbq beef pizza

- ½ **pound lean ground beef**
- ⅔ **cup prepared barbecue sauce**
- 1 **medium green bell pepper**
- 1 **(14-inch) prepared pizza crust**
- 3 **to 4 onion slices, rings separated**
- ½ **(2¼-ounce) can sliced black olives, drained**
- 1 **cup (4 ounces) shredded cheese (Colby and Monterey Jack mix)**

1. Preheat oven to 400°F. Place meat in large skillet; cook over high heat 6 to 8 minutes or until meat is no longer pink, breaking meat apart with wooden spoon. Pour off drippings; remove from heat. Stir in barbecue sauce.

2. While meat is cooking, seed bell pepper and slice into ¼-inch-thick rings. Place pizza crust on baking pan. Spread meat mixture over pizza crust to within ½ inch of edge. Arrange onion slices and pepper rings over meat. Sprinkle with olives and cheese. Bake 8 minutes or until cheese is melted. Cut into 8 wedges. *makes 3 to 4 servings*

prep and cook time: 20 minutes

golden chicken nuggets

1 pound boneless
  skinless chicken
  breasts, cut into
  1½-inch pieces

¼ cup *French's®* Honey
  Mustard

2 cups *French's® Taste
  Toppers™* French
  Fried Onions, finely
  crushed

1. Preheat oven to 400°F. Toss chicken with mustard in medium bowl.

2. Place *Taste Toppers* into resealable plastic food storage bag. Toss chicken in *Taste Toppers*, a few pieces at a time, pressing gently to adhere.

3. Place chicken in shallow baking pan. Bake 15 minutes or until chicken is no longer pink in center. Serve with additional honey mustard.

makes 4 servings

prep time: 5 minutes
cook time: 15 minutes

baked pasta and cheese supreme

8 ounces uncooked
  fusilli pasta

8 ounces uncooked
  bacon, diced

½ onion, chopped

2 cloves garlic, minced

2 teaspoons dried
  oregano, divided

1 can (8 ounces) tomato
  sauce

1 teaspoon hot pepper
  sauce (optional)

1½ cups (6 ounces)
  shredded Cheddar
  or Colby cheese

½ cup fresh bread
  crumbs (from 1 slice
  of white bread)

1 tablespoon melted
  butter

Preheat oven to 400°F. Cook pasta according to package directions; drain. Meanwhile, cook bacon in large ovenproof skillet over medium heat until crisp; drain.

Add onion, garlic and 1 teaspoon oregano to skillet; cook and stir about 3 minutes or until onion is tender. Stir in tomato sauce and hot pepper sauce. Add cooked pasta and cheese to skillet; stir to coat.

Combine bread crumbs, remaining 1 teaspoon oregano and melted butter in small bowl; sprinkle over pasta mixture. Bake about 5 minutes or until hot and bubbly. Garnish, if desired.

makes 4 servings

156

tuna quesadilla stack

4 (10-inch) flour
   tortillas, divided

¼ cup plus
   2 tablespoons pinto
   or black bean dip

1 can (9 ounces) tuna
   packed in water,
   drained and flaked

2 cups (8 ounces)
   shredded Cheddar
   cheese

1 can (14½ ounces)
   diced tomatoes,
   drained

½ cup thinly sliced
   green onions

½ tablespoon butter or
   margarine, melted

1. Preheat oven to 400°F.

2. Place 1 tortilla on 12-inch pizza pan. Spread with 2 tablespoons bean dip, leaving ½-inch border. Top with one third each of tuna, cheese, tomatoes and green onions. Repeat layers twice, beginning with tortilla and ending with onions.

3. Top with remaining tortilla, pressing gently. Brush with melted butter.

4. Bake 15 minutes or until cheese melts and top is lightly browned. Cool and cut into 8 wedges.   *makes 4 servings*

tip: For a special touch, serve with assorted toppings, such as guacamole, sour cream and salsa.

prep and cook time: 25 minutes

creamy broccoli and cheese

1 package (8 ounces)
   cream cheese,
   softened

¾ cup milk

1 packet (1 ounce)
   HIDDEN VALLEY®
   Original Ranch®
   Salad Dressing &
   Recipe Mix

1 pound fresh broccoli,
   cooked and drained

½ cup (2 ounces)
   shredded sharp
   Cheddar cheese

In a food processor fitted with a metal blade, blend cream cheese, milk and salad dressing & recipe mix until smooth. Pour over broccoli in a 9-inch baking dish; stir well. Top with cheese. Bake at 350°F for 25 minutes or until cheese is melted.   *makes 4 servings*

ham & barbecued bean skillet

1 tablespoon vegetable oil

1 cup chopped onion

1 teaspoon minced garlic

1 can (15 ounces) red or pink kidney beans, rinsed and drained

1 can (15 ounces) cannellini or Great Northern beans, rinsed and drained

1 cup chopped green bell pepper

½ cup firmly packed light brown sugar

½ cup catsup

2 tablespoons cider vinegar

2 teaspoons dry mustard

1 fully cooked smoked ham steak (about 12 ounces), cut ½ inch thick

1. Heat oil in large deep skillet over medium-high heat until hot. Add onion and garlic; cook 3 minutes, stirring occasionally.

2. Add kidney beans, cannellini beans, bell pepper, brown sugar, catsup, vinegar and mustard; mix well.

3. Trim fat from ham; cut into ½-inch pieces. Add ham to bean mixture; simmer over medium heat 5 minutes or until sauce thickens and mixture is heated through, stirring occasionally. *makes 4 servings*

serving suggestion: Serve with a Caesar salad and crisp breadsticks.

prep and cook time: 20 minutes

If you're using a garlic press to mince garlic, you don't need to peel the cloves before putting them through the press. When you squeeze a clove in the press, the garlic flesh will be forced through the holes while the skin stays behind in the press. (This also makes it easier to clean the press.)

pizza soup

- 2 cans (10¾ ounces each) condensed tomato soup
- ¾ teaspoon garlic powder
- ½ teaspoon dried oregano leaves
- ¾ cup uncooked tiny pasta shells (¼-inch)
- 1 cup shredded quick-melting mozzarella cheese
- 1 cup *French's*® *Taste Toppers*™ French Fried Onions

1. Combine soup, *2 soup cans of water*, garlic powder and oregano in small saucepan. Bring to boiling over medium-high heat.

2. Add pasta. Cook 8 minutes or until pasta is tender.

3. Stir in cheese. Cook until cheese melts. Sprinkle with *Taste Toppers*.

makes 4 servings

prep time: 5 minutes
cook time: 10 minutes

original ortega® taco recipe

- 1 pound ground beef
- ¾ cup water
- 1 package (1¼ ounces) ORTEGA® Taco Seasoning Mix
- 1 package (12) ORTEGA® Taco Shells, warmed
- Toppings: shredded lettuce, chopped tomatoes, shredded mild Cheddar cheese, ORTEGA® Thick & Smooth Taco Sauce

BROWN beef; drain, Stir in water and seasoning mix. Bring to a boil. Reduce heat to low; cook, stirring occasionally, for 5 to 6 minutes or until mixture is thickened.

FILL taco shells with beef mixture. Top with lettuce, tomatoes, cheese and taco sauce.

makes 6 servings

161

salsa macaroni & cheese

- 1 jar (16 ounces) RAGÚ® Cheese Creations!® Double Cheddar Sauce
- 1 cup prepared mild salsa
- 8 ounces elbow macaroni, cooked and drained

1. In 2-quart saucepan, heat Ragú Cheese Creations! Sauce over medium heat. Stir in salsa; heat through.

2. Toss with hot macaroni. Serve immediately. *makes 4 servings*

prep time: 5 minutes
cook time: 15 minutes

french bread pizza

- ½ pound bulk Italian turkey sausage
- ½ pound extra lean ground beef
- 1 (15½-ounce) can HUNT'S® Manwich Sloppy Joe Sauce
- 2 tablespoons grated Parmesan cheese
- 1 teaspoon dried oregano
- 1 (16-ounce) loaf unsliced French bread
- 1 cup shredded fat-free mozzarella cheese

1. In large skillet, brown sausage with beef; drain. Stir in Manwich Sauce, Parmesan cheese and oregano. Simmer, uncovered, for 5 minutes.

2. Halve bread lengthwise. Top *each* half loaf with *half* of meat mixture and mozzarella cheese.

3. Place on baking sheet and broil 5 to 6 inches from heat source for 3 minutes or until hot and bubbly. Cut into 16 slices.

makes 16 servings

oven "fries"

2 small baking potatoes (10 ounces)

2 teaspoons olive oil

¼ teaspoon salt or onion salt

1. Preheat oven to 450°F. Peel potatoes and cut lengthwise into ¼-inch strips. Place in colander; rinse under cold running water and drain well. Pat dry with paper towels. Place potatoes in small resealable plastic food storage bag. Drizzle with oil. Seal bag; shake to coat potatoes with oil.

2. Arrange potatoes in single layer on baking sheet. Bake 20 to 25 minutes or until light brown and crisp. Sprinkle with salt or onion salt.

makes 2 servings

stromboli

1 package (10 ounces) refrigerated pizza dough

⅓ cup *French's*® Deli Brown Mustard

¾ pound sliced deli meats and cheese such as salami, provolone cheese and ham

1 egg, beaten

1 teaspoon poppy or sesame seeds

1. Preheat oven to 425°F. Unroll pizza dough on lightly floured board. Roll into 13×10-inch rectangle. Spread mustard evenly on dough. Layer luncheon meats and cheeses on dough, overlapping slices, leaving a 1-inch border around edges.

2. Fold one-third of dough toward center from long edge of rectangle. Fold second side toward center enclosing filling. Pinch long edge to seal. Pinch ends together and tuck under dough. Place on greased baking sheet.

3. Cut shallow crosswise slits on top of dough, spacing 3 inches apart. Brush stromboli lightly with beaten egg; sprinkle with poppy seeds. Bake 15 to 18 minutes or until deep golden brown. Remove to rack; cool slightly. Serve warm.

makes 12 servings

prep time: 20 minutes
cook time: 15 minutes

hot dog burritos

1 can (16 ounces) pork and beans

⅓ cup ketchup

2 tablespoons *French's®* Classic Yellow® Mustard

2 tablespoons brown sugar

8 frankfurters, cooked

8 (8-inch) flour tortillas, heated

1. Combine beans, ketchup, mustard and brown sugar in medium saucepan. Bring to boiling over medium-high heat. Reduce heat to low and simmer 2 minutes.

2. Arrange frankfurters in heated tortillas and top with bean mixture. Roll up jelly-roll style.

makes 8 servings

tip: Try topping dogs with *French's® Taste Toppers™* before rolling up!

prep time: 5 minutes
cook time: 8 minutes

tamale pie

1 tablespoon olive or vegetable oil

1 small onion, chopped

1 pound ground beef

1 envelope LIPTON® RECIPE SECRETS® Onion Soup Mix*

1 can (14½ ounces) stewed tomatoes, undrained

½ cup water

1 can (15 to 19 ounces) red kidney beans, rinsed and drained

1 package (8½ ounces) corn muffin mix

• Preheat oven to 400°F.

• In 12-inch skillet, heat oil over medium heat and cook onion, stirring occasionally, 3 minutes or until tender. Stir in ground beef and cook until browned.

• Stir in onion soup mix blended with tomatoes and water. Bring to a boil over high heat, stirring with spoon to crush tomatoes. Reduce heat to low and stir in beans. Simmer uncovered, stirring occasionally, 10 minutes. Turn into 2-quart casserole.

• Prepare corn muffin mix according to package directions. Spoon evenly over casserole.

• Bake uncovered 15 minutes or until corn topping is golden and filling is hot.

makes about 6 servings

Also terrific with LIPTON® RECIPE SECRETS® Fiesta Herb with Red Pepper, Onion-Mushroom, Beefy Onion or Beefy Mushroom Soup Mix.

hot dog burrito

original ranch® roasted potatoes

2 pounds small red potatoes, quartered

¼ cup vegetable oil

1 packet (1 ounce) HIDDEN VALLEY® Original Ranch® Salad Dressing & Recipe Mix

Place potatoes in a gallon-size Glad® Zipper Storage Bag. Pour oil over potatoes. Seal bag and toss to coat. Add salad dressing & recipe mix; seal bag and toss again until coated. Bake in ungreased baking pan at 450°F for 30 to 35 minutes or until potatoes are brown and crisp.

makes 4 to 6 servings

tuna supper sandwiches

2 cups shredded Cheddar cheese

⅓ cup chopped green onions, including tops

⅓ cup chopped red bell pepper

1 can (2¼ ounces) sliced ripe olives, drained

2 tablespoons minced fresh parsley

1 teaspoon curry powder

Seasoned salt to taste

1 can (12 ounces) STARKIST® Solid White or Chunk Light Tuna, drained and chunked

½ cup light mayonnaise

6 soft French rolls (7 inches *each*), halved lengthwise

In medium bowl, place cheese, onions, red pepper, olives, parsley, curry powder and salt; mix lightly. Add tuna and mayonnaise; toss lightly with fork. Cover baking sheet with foil; place rolls on foil. Spread about ⅓ cup mixture on each half. Bake in 450°F oven 10 to 12 minutes or until tops are bubbling and beginning to brown. Cool slightly before serving.

makes 12 servings

prep time: 18 minutes
cook time: 12 minutes

168

santa fe chicken & pasta

1 jar (12 ounces) mild chunky salsa

1 can (10¾ ounces) condensed Cheddar cheese soup

¾ cup sour cream

5 cups hot cooked ziti pasta (8 ounces uncooked)

1⅓ cups *French's*® Taste Toppers™ French Fried Onions, divided

1 package (10 ounces) fully cooked carved chicken breast (2 cups cut-up chicken)

1 cup (4 ounces) cubed Monterey Jack cheese with jalapeño

1. Preheat oven to 375°F. In large bowl, mix salsa, soup and sour cream. Stir in pasta, ⅔ *cup* **Taste Toppers**, chicken and cheese; mix well. Spoon into 3-quart casserole.

2. Cover; bake 40 minutes or until hot and bubbly. Stir.

3. Sprinkle with remaining ⅔ *cup* **Taste Toppers**. Bake 3 minutes or until **Taste Toppers** are golden.   *makes 8 servings*

prep time: 10 minutes
cook time: 43 minutes

When cooking pasta for a casserole, don't cook it as long as the package recommends. Reduce the cooking time by about one-third, as the pasta will continue to cook and absorb liquid when the casserole goes in the oven.

minestrone soup with mini meatballs

1 pound ground beef or ground turkey

1 teaspoon dried Italian seasoning

½ teaspoon garlic powder, divided

2 tablespoons vegetable oil, divided

5 cups assorted fresh vegetables*

1 envelope LIPTON® RECIPE SECRETS® Onion Soup Mix

4 cups water

1 can (28 ounces) Italian plum tomatoes, undrained

1 teaspoon sugar

*Use any of the following to equal 5 cups: green beans, cut into 1-inch pieces; diced zucchini; diced carrot; or diced celery.

In medium bowl, combine ground beef, Italian seasoning and ¼ teaspoon garlic powder. Shape into 1-inch meatballs.

In 6-quart Dutch oven or heavy saucepan, heat 1 tablespoon oil over medium-high heat and brown meatballs. Remove meatballs. Heat remaining 1 tablespoon oil in same Dutch oven and cook vegetables, stirring frequently, 5 minutes or until crisp-tender. Stir in soup mix blended with water, remaining ¼ teaspoon garlic powder, tomatoes and sugar. Bring to a boil over high heat, breaking up tomatoes with wooden spoon. Reduce heat to low and simmer covered 25 minutes. Return meatballs to skillet. Continue simmering covered 5 minutes or until meatballs are heated through. Serve with grated Parmesan cheese and garlic bread, if desired. *makes 6 servings*

chicken parmesan hero sandwiches

4 boneless, skinless chicken breast halves (about 1¼ pounds)

1 egg, slightly beaten

¾ cup Italian seasoned dry bread crumbs

1 jar (26 to 28 ounces) RAGÚ® Old World Style® Pasta Sauce

1 cup shredded mozzarella cheese (about 4 ounces)

4 long Italian rolls, halved lengthwise

1. Preheat oven to 400°F. Dip chicken in egg, then bread crumbs, coating well.

2. In 13×9-inch glass baking dish, arrange chicken. Bake uncovered 20 minutes.

3. Pour Ragú Pasta Sauce over chicken, then top with cheese. Bake an additional 10 minutes or until chicken is no longer pink. To serve, arrange chicken and sauce on rolls. *makes 4 servings*

prep time: 10 minutes
cook time: 30 minutes

easy kids' taco-mac

1 pound ground turkey

1 package (1.0 ounce) LAWRY'S® Taco Spices & Seasonings

1 can (14½ ounces) whole peeled tomatoes, undrained and cut up

1 cup water

8 ounces dry macaroni or small spiral pasta

½ cup sliced celery

1 package (8½ ounces) corn muffin mix

1 egg

⅓ cup milk

In medium skillet, brown ground turkey until crumbly. Add Taco Spices & Seasonings, tomatoes, water, pasta and celery; mix well. Bring to a boil over medium-high heat; reduce heat to low and simmer covered 20 minutes. In medium bowl, combine corn muffin mix, egg and milk; stir with fork just to mix. Place turkey mixture in 2½-quart casserole dish. Spoon dollops of corn muffin mix on top. Bake in 400°F oven 15 to 20 minutes or until golden. *makes 6 to 8 servings*

serving suggestion: Sprinkle with grated cheese.

172

by-the-sea casserole

- **1 bag (16 ounces) BIRDS EYE® frozen Mixed Vegetables**
- **2 cans (6 ounces each) tuna in water, drained**
- **1 cup uncooked instant rice**
- **1 can (10¾ ounces) cream of celery soup**
- **1 cup 1% milk**
- **1 cup cheese-flavored fish-shaped crackers**

- In medium bowl, combine vegetables and tuna.

- Stir in rice, soup and milk.

- Place tuna mixture in 1½-quart microwave-safe casserole dish; cover and microwave on HIGH 6 minutes. Stir; microwave, covered, 6 to 8 minutes more or until rice is tender.

- Stir casserole and sprinkle with crackers.   *makes 6 servings*

birds eye idea: Need to cut salt out of your diet? Add spices and herbs instead.

prep time: 10 minutes
cook time: 15 minutes

souper quick "lasagna"

- **1½ pounds ground beef**
- **1 envelope LIPTON® RECIPE SECRETS® Onion or Onion-Mushroom Soup Mix**
- **3 cans (8 ounces each) tomato sauce**
- **1 cup water**
- **½ teaspoon dried oregano leaves (optional)**
- **1 package (8 ounces) broad egg noodles, cooked and drained**
- **1 package (16 ounces) mozzarella cheese, shredded**

Preheat oven to 375°F.

In 12-inch skillet, brown ground beef over medium-high heat; drain. Stir in onion soup mix, tomato sauce, water and oregano. Simmer covered, stirring occasionally, 15 minutes.

In 2-quart oblong baking dish spoon enough sauce to cover bottom. Alternately layer noodles, ground beef mixture and cheese, ending with cheese. Bake 30 minutes or until bubbling.   *makes about 6 servings*

microwave directions: In 2-quart casserole, microwave ground beef, uncovered, at HIGH (Full Power) 7 minutes, stirring once; drain. Stir in onion soup mix, tomato sauce, water and oregano. Microwave at MEDIUM (50% Power) 5 minutes, stirring once. In 2-quart oblong baking dish, spoon enough sauce to cover bottom. Alternately layer as above. Microwave covered at MEDIUM, turning dish occasionally, 10 minutes or until bubbling. Let stand covered 5 minutes.

174

hot diggity dots & twisters

⅔ cup milk

2 tablespoons margarine or butter

1 (4.8-ounce) package PASTA RONI® Four Cheese Flavor with Corkscrew Pasta

1½ cups frozen peas

4 hot dogs, cut into ½-inch pieces

2 teaspoons mustard

1. In large saucepan, bring 1¼ cups water, milk and margarine just to a boil.

2. Stir in pasta, peas and Special Seasonings; return to a boil. Reduce heat to medium. Gently boil uncovered, 7 to 8 minutes or until pasta is tender, stirring occasionally.

3. Stir in hot dogs and mustard. Let stand 3 to 5 minutes before serving.

makes 4 servings

prep time: 5 minutes
cook time: 15 minutes

chicken rice casserole

4 tablespoons butter, divided

4 boneless skinless chicken breasts

1½ cups uncooked converted rice

6 ounces HILLSHIRE FARM® Lit'l Smokies

1 can (about 14 ounces) cream of chicken soup

1 can (about 14 ounces) cream of celery soup

1 cup sliced mushrooms

½ cup dry sherry

Bread crumbs

Cheddar cheese

Slivered almonds

Preheat oven to 275°F.

Melt 2 tablespoons butter in large skillet over medium-high heat. Add chicken; sauté until cooked through, about 7 minutes on each side. Remove chicken and cut into bite-size pieces.

Place rice on bottom of medium casserole; add chicken, Lit'l Smokies, soups, ¾ cup water, mushrooms, sherry and remaining 2 tablespoons butter. Bake, covered, 2½ hours. Top casserole with bread crumbs, cheese and almonds. Broil until golden brown and cheese is melted.

makes 6 to 8 servings

tip: Be sure to avoid overcooking—it's the major pitfall of casseroles destined for the freezer. A simple way is to undercook any pasta or rice; it will cook through when the casserole is reheated.

chuckwagon bbq rice round-up

1 pound lean ground beef

1 (6.8-ounce) package RICE-A-RONI® Beef Flavor

2 tablespoons margarine or butter

2 cups frozen corn

½ cup prepared barbecue sauce

½ cup (2 ounces) shredded Cheddar cheese

1. In large skillet over medium-high heat, brown ground beef until well cooked. Remove from skillet; drain. Set aside.

2. In same skillet over medium heat, sauté rice-vermicelli mix with margarine until vermicelli is golden brown.

3. Slowly stir in 2½ cups water, corn and Special Seasonings; bring to a boil. Reduce heat to low. Cover; simmer 15 to 20 minutes or until rice is tender.

4. Stir in barbecue sauce and ground beef. Sprinkle with cheese. Cover; let stand 3 to 5 minutes or until cheese is melted.

makes 4 servings

tip: Salsa can be substituted for barbecue sauce.

prep time: 5 minutes
cook time: 25 minutes

funny face pizzas

1 package (10 ounces) refrigerated pizza dough

1 cup pizza sauce

1 cup (4 ounces) shredded mozzarella cheese

Assorted toppings: pepperoni, black olive slices, green or red bell pepper slices, mushroom slices

⅓ cup shredded Cheddar cheese

Heat oven to 425°F. Spray baking sheet with nonstick cooking spray; set aside.

Remove dough from package. *Do not unroll dough.* Slice dough into 4 equal pieces. Knead each piece of dough until ball forms. Pat or roll each ball into 4-inch disk. Place disks on prepared baking sheet.

Spread ¼ cup sauce on each disk. Sprinkle with mozzarella cheese. Decorate with toppings to create faces. Sprinkle with Cheddar cheese to resemble hair.

Bake 10 minutes or until cheese is just melted and bottoms of pizzas are light brown.

makes 4 servings

Contents

Fudgy Milk Chocolate Fondue

1 (16-ounce) can chocolate-flavored syrup
1 (14-ounce) can EAGLE BRAND® Sweetened Condensed Milk (NOT evaporated milk)
Dash salt
1½ teaspoons vanilla extract
Assorted dippers: cookies, cake, pound cake cubes, angel food cake cubes, banana chunks, apple slices, strawberries, pear slices, kiwifruit slices and/or marshmallows

1. In heavy saucepan over medium heat, combine syrup, Eagle Brand and salt. Cook and stir 12 to 15 minutes or until slightly thickened.

2. Remove from heat; stir in vanilla. Serve warm with assorted dippers. Store covered in refrigerator. *Makes about 3 cups*

Microwave Directions: In 1-quart glass measure, combine syrup, Eagle Brand and salt. Microwave at HIGH (100% power) 3½ to 4 minutes, stirring after 2 minutes. Stir in vanilla.

Tip: Can be served warm or cold over ice cream. Can be made several weeks ahead. Store tightly covered in refrigerator.

Prep Time: 12 to 15 minutes

Fudgy Milk Chocolate Fondue

Golden Artichoke Dip

1 envelope LIPTON® RECIPE SECRETS® Golden Onion Soup Mix*
1 can (14 ounces) artichoke hearts, drained and chopped
1 cup HELLMANN'S® or BEST FOODS® Real Mayonnaise
1 container (8 ounces) sour cream
1 cup shredded Swiss or mozzarella cheese (about 4 ounces)

*Also terrific with LIPTON® RECIPE SECRETS® Savory Herb with Garlic or Onion Soup Mix.

1. Preheat oven to 350°F. In 1-quart casserole, combine all ingredients.

2. Bake uncovered 30 minutes or until heated through.

3. Serve with your favorite dippers.

Makes 3 cups dip

Variation: For a cold artichoke dip, omit Swiss cheese. Stir in, if desired, ¼ cup grated Parmesan cheese. Do not bake.

Recipe Tip: For a quick party fix or anytime treat, try these CLASSIC LIPTON DIPS: Combine 1 envelope Lipton Recipe Secrets Onion, Ranch, Savory Herb with Garlic, Onion Mushroom, Beefy Onion, Beefy Mushroom, Golden Onion or Vegetable Soup Mix with 1 container (16 ounces) sour cream. Chill and serve with your favorite dippers.

182

Heavenly Nonfat Chocolate Honey Dip

1 cup nonfat sour cream
½ cup honey
½ cup unsweetened cocoa powder
1 teaspoon vanilla

Combine all ingredients in medium bowl until well blended. Cover and refrigerate until ready to serve. Serve with assorted fruits and chunks of angel food cake.   *Makes about 1½ cups*

Favorite recipe from **National Honey Board**

Bananas & Cheesecake Dipping Sauce

½ cup sour cream
2 ounces cream cheese
2 tablespoons plus 1 teaspoon fat-free (skim) milk
2 tablespoons sugar
½ teaspoon vanilla
   Nutmeg (optional)
6 medium bananas, unpeeled and cut crosswise into halves *or* 6 red bananas

Place all ingredients except bananas in blender and blend until smooth. Pour 2 tablespoons sauce into each of 6 small plastic containers; sprinkle with nutmeg, if desired. Cover tightly. Refrigerate until needed or place containers in small cooler with ice.

To serve, partially peel banana and dip directly into sauce; continue to peel and dip.

Makes 6 servings

Tropical Coconut Cream Dipping Sauce: Substitute coconut extract for vanilla.

184

Orange Yogurt Dip for Fresh Fruit

1 carton (8 ounces) low-fat plain yogurt
2 tablespoons honey
   Grated peel of ½ SUNKIST® orange
2 SUNKIST® oranges, peeled and segmented
1 medium unpeeled apple, sliced*
1 medium banana, peeled and cut into chunks*

*Sprinkle cut apple and banana with small amount of orange or lemon juice to prevent fruit from darkening.

In small bowl, combine yogurt, honey and orange peel. Serve as dip with oranges, apple and banana.

Makes 4 (2-ounce) servings

Tip: To serve in orange shells, cut oranges in half crosswise in middle. Ream juice from both halves. Scrape shells clean with spoon. Cut small slice off bottom of shells so oranges sit flat. Fill as desired. Shells can be made and frozen ahead, to be used at a later date. (Save juice for drinking or use in other recipes.)

Bananas & Cheesecake Dipping Sauce

Warm Peanut-Caramel Dip

¼ cup peanut butter
2 tablespoons caramel topping
2 tablespoons fat-free (skim) milk
1 large apple, thinly sliced
4 large pretzel rods, broken in half

1. Combine peanut butter, caramel topping and milk in small saucepan. Heat over low heat, stirring constantly, until mixture is melted and warm.

2. Serve dip with apple and pretzel rods.

Makes 4 servings

Microwave Directions: Combine peanut butter, caramel topping and milk in small microwavable dish. Microwave at MEDIUM (50%) 1 minute; stir well. Microwave an additional minute or until mixture is melted and warm. Serve dip with apple and pretzel rods.

186

Dipsy Doodles Butterscotch Dip

1 (14-ounce) can EAGLE BRAND® Sweetened Condensed Milk (NOT evaporated milk)
1½ cups milk
1 (4-serving-size) package cook-and-serve butterscotch pudding and pie filling mix
  Apples or pears, cored and sliced, or banana chunks

1. In medium saucepan over medium heat, combine Eagle Brand, milk and pudding mix. Cook and stir until thickened and bubbly; cook 2 minutes more.

2. Cool slightly. Pour into serving bowl or individual cups. Serve warm with fruit.

Makes about 2½ cups dip

Tip: Store leftovers covered in the refrigerator. Reheat and serve as a sauce over vanilla ice cream. Sprinkle sauce with miniature semi-sweet chocolate chips or toasted nuts, if desired.

Prep Time: 15 minutes

Warm Peanut-Caramel Dip

White Pizza Dip

1 envelope LIPTON® RECIPE SECRETS® Savory Herb with Garlic Soup Mix
1 container (16 ounces) sour cream
1 cup (8 ounces) ricotta cheese
1 cup shredded mozzarella cheese (about 4 ounces)
¼ cup (1 ounce) chopped pepperoni (optional)
1 loaf Italian or French bread, sliced

1. Preheat oven to 350°F. In shallow 1-quart casserole, combine soup mix, sour cream, ricotta cheese, ¾ cup mozzarella cheese and pepperoni.

2. Sprinkle with remaining ¼ cup mozzarella cheese.

3. Bake uncovered 30 minutes or until heated through. Serve with bread.

Makes 3 cups dip

Prep Time: 10 minutes
Cook Time: 30 minutes

Chocolate-Caramel Fondue

3 (1-ounce) squares unsweetened chocolate, chopped
1 (14-ounce) can EAGLE BRAND® Sweetened Condensed Milk (NOT evaporated milk)
1 (12¼-ounce) jar caramel ice cream topping
   Dippers: Fresh fruit, cookies, pound cake pieces or angel food cake pieces

1. In medium saucepan, melt chocolate with Eagle Brand and caramel topping.

2. Pour into serving bowl or individual cups. Serve with desired dippers.

Makes 2½ cups

Prep Time: 15 minutes

Chocolate Fruit Dip

1 container (8 ounces) vanilla lowfat yogurt
⅓ cup packed light brown sugar
1 tablespoon HERSHEY'S Cocoa
½ teaspoon vanilla extract
Dash ground cinnamon
Assorted fresh fruit, cut up

1. Combine all ingredients except fruit in small bowl; stir with whisk until smooth. Cover; refrigerate until well chilled. Serve with assorted fresh fruit. Cover and refrigerate leftover dip.

Makes 10 servings

Peanut Butter Fruit Dip

190

2 cups skim milk
½ cup light sour cream
1 (3.4-ounce) package vanilla instant pudding and pie filling mix
1 cup JIF® Reduced Fat Peanut Butter
⅓ cup sugar
Apple and banana slices (or any fruit of your choice)

Combine milk, sour cream and pudding mix in medium bowl. Whisk until smooth. Stir peanut butter until evenly mixed throughout; measure after stirring. Stir peanut butter and sugar into pudding mixture; mix until well blended.

Serve with sliced apples or bananas. Store in refrigerator. If dip becomes too thick, stir in additional milk.

Makes 3 cups

Tip: Try stirring in ¼ cup SMUCKER'S® Hot Fudge Ice Cream Topping to make a rich peanut butter and chocolate dessert dip.

Chocolate Fruit Dip

Pizza Fondue

½ pound bulk Italian sausage
1 cup chopped onion
2 jars (26 ounces each) meatless pasta sauce
4 ounces thinly sliced ham, finely chopped
1 package (3 ounces) sliced pepperoni, finely chopped
¼ teaspoon red pepper flakes
1 pound mozzarella cheese, cut into ¾-inch cubes
1 loaf Italian or French bread, cut into 1-inch cubes

SLOW COOKER DIRECTIONS

1. Cook sausage and onion in large skillet until sausage is browned. Drain off fat.

2. Transfer sausage mixture to slow cooker. Stir in pasta sauce, ham, pepperoni and pepper flakes. Cover; cook on LOW 3 to 4 hours.

3. Serve fondue with cheese cubes, bread cubes and fondue forks.

Makes 20 to 25 appetizer servings

192

Prep Time: 15 minutes
Cook Time: 3 to 4 hours

Peanutty Banana Dip

½ cup sliced bananas
⅓ cup reduced-fat creamy peanut butter
2 tablespoons fat-free (skim) milk
1 tablespoon honey
½ teaspoon vanilla
⅛ teaspoon ground cinnamon

Place all ingredients in blender and process until smooth.

Makes ¾ cup

Tip: Try this dip with Granny Smith apple slices or celery sticks.

Dreamy Orange Cheesecake Dip

1 package (8 ounces) reduced-fat cream cheese, softened
½ cup orange marmalade
½ teaspoon vanilla
  Grated orange peel (optional)
  Mint leaves (optional)
2 cups whole strawberries
2 cups cantaloupe chunks
2 cups apple slices

1. Combine cream cheese, marmalade and vanilla in small bowl; mix well. Garnish with orange peel and mint leaves, if desired.

2. Serve with fruit dippers.

Makes 12 servings

Note: Dip may be prepared ahead of time. Store, covered, in refrigerator for up to 2 days.

194

Party Pizza Spread

2 packages (8 ounces each) cream cheese, softened
1 packet (1 ounce) HIDDEN VALLEY® The Original Ranch® Salad Dressing & Seasoning Mix
½ teaspoon minced garlic
½ teaspoon dried rosemary, crushed
1 cup chili sauce
½ cup chopped green onions
1 cup shredded Monterey Jack cheese
½ cup mushroom slices, olives, ham, green pepper, or any favorite pizza topping

In large bowl, blend cream cheese, salad dressing & seasoning mix, garlic and rosemary until smooth. Spread into 10-inch circle on serving platter, smoothing mixture with spatula. Pour chili sauce over cream cheese mixture into 9-inch circle, creating "cheese crust" border. Sprinkle with green onions, cheese and toppings. Refrigerate at least 30 minutes before serving. Serve with crackers for dipping.

Makes 8 to 10 servings

Dreamy Orange Cheesecake Dip

7-Layer Ranch Dip

1 envelope LIPTON® RECIPE SECRETS® Ranch Soup Mix
1 container (16 ounces) sour cream
1 cup shredded lettuce
1 medium tomato, chopped (about 1 cup)
1 can (2.25 ounces) sliced pitted ripe olives, drained
¼ cup chopped red onion
1 can (4.5 ounces) chopped green chilies, drained
1 cup shredded Cheddar cheese (about 4 ounces)

1. In 2-quart shallow dish, combine soup mix and sour cream.

2. Evenly layer remaining ingredients, ending with cheese. Chill, if desired. Serve with tortilla chips.

Makes 7 cups dip

Prep Time: 15 minutes

Savory Peanut Butter Dip

¼ cup creamy peanut butter
3 ounces fat-free cream cheese
1 to 2 tablespoons lemon or apple juice
½ teaspoon ground cinnamon
⅛ to ¼ cup natural applesauce
2 apples, sliced
1 small banana, sliced
   Celery stalks, sliced into 4-inch pieces
2 cups broccoli flowerets

Combine peanut butter, cream cheese, lemon juice and cinnamon in food processor. Process until smooth. Add applesauce gradually to reach desired consistency for dip. Chill before serving with fresh fruits and vegetables. Or, try serving dip over baked sweet potatoes.

Makes about 8 servings

Favorite recipe from **Peanut Advisory Board**

7-Layer Ranch Dip

Cookie Fondue

COOKIE DIPPERS
1 package (18 ounces) refrigerated oatmeal raisin cookie dough
1 egg
1 cup powdered sugar

CHOCOLATE SAUCE
½ cup semisweet chocolate chips
¼ cup heavy cream

WHITE CHOCOLATE SAUCE
½ cup white chocolate chips
¼ cup heavy cream

STRAWBERRY-MARSHMALLOW SAUCE
¼ cup strawberry syrup
¼ cup marshmallow creme

198

1. For cookie dippers, preheat oven to 350°F. Grease cookie sheets. Remove dough from wrapper; place in large bowl. Let dough stand at room temperature about 15 minutes.

2. Add egg and powdered sugar to dough in bowl; beat at medium speed of electric mixer until well blended. Drop dough by teaspoonfuls onto prepared cookie sheets.

3. Bake 8 minutes or until slightly brown at edges. Cool on cookie sheet 5 minutes; remove to wire racks to cool completely.

4. For chocolate sauce, combine semisweet chocolate chips and cream in microwavable bowl. Heat at HIGH (100% power) 20 seconds; stir. Heat at HIGH for additional 20-second intervals until chips are melted and mixture is smooth; stir well after each 20-second interval.

5. For white chocolate sauce, combine white chocolate chips and cream in microwavable bowl. Heat at HIGH (100% power) 20 seconds; stir. Heat at HIGH for additional 20-second intervals until chips are melted and mixture is smooth; stir well after each 20-second interval.

6. For strawberry-marshmallow sauce, combine strawberry syrup and marshmallow creme in small bowl; stir until smooth.

7. Serve cookie dippers with sauces.   *Makes 2½ dozen cookies*

Tip: Serve sauces in small bowls along with small bowls of chopped nuts, coconut and dried cranberries for "double" dipping.

Ortega® Green Chile Guacamole

2 medium very ripe avocados, seeded, peeled and mashed
1 can (4 ounces) ORTEGA® Diced Green Chiles
2 large green onions, chopped
2 tablespoons olive oil
1 teaspoon lime juice
1 clove garlic, finely chopped
¼ teaspoon salt
Tortilla chips

COMBINE avocados, chiles, green onions, olive oil, lime juice, garlic and salt in medium bowl. Cover; refrigerate for at least 1 hour. Serve with chips. *Makes 2 cups*

Tip: This all-time favorite dip can be used in tacos, burritos, tamales, chimichangas or combined with ORTEGA Salsa for a spicy salad dressing.

200

Peanut Spice Dip

1 (8-ounce) container lite non-dairy whipped topping
½ cup firmly packed light brown sugar
¼ cup PETER PAN® Honey Roasted Creamy Peanut Butter
1 teaspoon ground cinnamon
½ teaspoon vanilla
¼ teaspoon ground allspice
¼ teaspoon ground nutmeg
Assorted fresh fruit, cut into bite-size pieces
Angel food cake or pound cake, cut into bite-size pieces

In small bowl, combine whipped topping, sugar, peanut butter, cinnamon, vanilla, allspice and nutmeg; blend well. Cover and refrigerate at least 20 minutes or until ready to serve. Serve with fresh fruit in season and/or cake. *Makes 1½ cups dip*

Prep Time: 7 minutes
Chill Time: 20 minutes

Ortega® Green Chile Guacamole

Chocolate Peanut Butter Fondue

⅓ **cup sugar**
⅓ **cup unsweetened cocoa powder**
⅓ **cup low-fat (1%) milk**
3 **tablespoons light corn syrup**
2 **tablespoons reduced-fat peanut butter**
½ **teaspoon vanilla**
2 **medium bananas, cut into 1-inch pieces**
16 **large strawberries**
2 **medium apples, cored, sliced**

1. Mix sugar, cocoa, milk, corn syrup and peanut butter in medium saucepan. Cook over medium heat, stirring constantly, until hot. Remove from heat; stir in vanilla.

2. Pour fondue into medium serving bowl; serve warm or at room temperature with fruit for dipping.

Makes 8 servings

202

Warm Broccoli 'n' Cheddar Dip

1 **envelope LIPTON® RECIPE SECRETS® Onion or Savory Herb with Garlic Soup Mix**
1 **container (16 ounces) sour cream**
1 **package (10 ounces) frozen chopped broccoli or spinach, thawed and squeezed dry**
1 **cup shredded Cheddar cheese (about 4 ounces)**

1. Preheat oven to 350°F. In 1-quart casserole, combine soup mix, sour cream, broccoli and ¾ cup cheese. Sprinkle with remaining ¼ cup cheese.

2. Bake uncovered 30 minutes or until heated through.

3. Serve with your favorite dippers.

Makes 3 cups dip

Chocolate Peanut Butter Fondue

Dipped, Drizzled & Decorated Pretzels

1 package (11 to 12 ounces) chocolate or flavored chips (choose semisweet, bittersweet, milk chocolate, green mint, white chocolate, butterscotch, peanut butter or a combination)
1 bag pretzel rods
   Assorted toppings: sprinkles, chopped nuts, coconut, toasted coconut, cookie crumbs, colored sugars (optional)

MICROWAVE DIRECTIONS

1. Place chips in microwavable bowl. (Be sure bowl and utensils are completely dry.) Cover with plastic wrap and turn back one corner to vent. Microwave at HIGH (100%) 1 minute; stir. Continue cooking in 30-second intervals until chips are completely melted, stirring after each heating.

2. Dip one half of each pretzel rod into melted chips. Roll coated end of several pretzels in toppings, if desired. Drizzle some pretzels with contrasting color or flavor melted chips. (Drizzle melted chocolate with spoon while rotating pretzel to cover pretzel evenly.)

3. Place decorated pretzels on wire rack; set rack over baking sheet lined with waxed-paper. Let coating harden completely. Do not refrigerate. *Makes about 2 dozen pretzels*

204

Banana Split Cups

    1 package (18 ounces) refrigerated chocolate chip cookie dough
⅔ cup "M&M's"® Chocolate Mini Baking Bits, divided
    1 ripe medium banana, cut into 18 slices and halved
    ¾ cup chocolate syrup, divided
2¼ cups any flavor ice cream, softened
      Aerosol whipped topping
    ¼ cup chopped maraschino cherries

Lightly grease 36 (1¾-inch) mini muffin cups. Cut dough into 36 equal pieces; roll into balls. Place 1 ball in bottom of each muffin cup. Press dough onto bottoms and up sides of muffin cups; chill 15 minutes. Press ⅓ cup "M&M's"® Chocolate Mini Baking Bits into bottoms and sides of dough cups. Preheat oven to 350°F. Bake cookies 8 to 9 minutes. Cookies will be puffy. Remove from oven; gently press down center of each cookie. Return to oven 1 minute. Cool cookies in muffin cups 5 minutes. Remove to wire racks; cool completely. Place 1 banana half slice in each cookie cup; top with ½ teaspoon chocolate syrup. Place about ½ teaspoon "M&M's"® Chocolate Mini Baking Bits in each cookie cup; top with 1 tablespoon ice cream. Top each cookie cup with ½ teaspoon chocolate syrup, whipped topping, remaining "M&M's"® Chocolate Mini Baking Bits and 1 maraschino cherry piece. Store covered in freezer.

Makes 3 dozen cookies

Rocky Road Sandwiches

1 package (18 ounces) refrigerated chocolate chip cookie dough
¼ cup unsweetened cocoa powder
1 cup marshmallow creme
⅔ cup (6 ounces) cream cheese, softened
1 cup finely chopped nuts

1. Preheat oven to 350°F. Grease cookie sheets.

2. Remove dough from wrapper; place in large bowl. Let dough stand at room temperature about 15 minutes.

3. Add cocoa to dough in bowl; beat at medium speed of electric mixer until well blended. Drop by rounded teaspoonfuls onto prepared cookie sheets.

4. Bake 8 to 10 minutes or until dough is set and cookies are no longer shiny. Transfer to wire racks to cool completely.

5. For filling, combine marshmallow creme and cream cheese in medium bowl; beat at medium speed of electric mixer until well blended. Place 1 tablespoon filling on flat side of cookie. Top with second cookie; press down to allow filling to squeeze out slightly between cookies. Roll filled edge in chopped nuts. Repeat with remaining cookies.

Makes about 1½ dozen sandwich cookies

Rocky Road Sandwiches

Cinnamon Stars

 2 tablespoons sugar
¾ teaspoon ground cinnamon
¾ cup butter or margarine, softened
 2 egg yolks
 1 teaspoon vanilla extract
 1 package DUNCAN HINES® Moist Deluxe® French Vanilla Cake Mix

1. Preheat oven to 375°F. Combine sugar and cinnamon in small bowl. Set aside.

2. Combine butter, egg yolks and vanilla extract in large bowl. Blend in cake mix gradually. Roll dough to ⅛-inch thickness on lightly floured surface. Cut with 2½-inch star cookie cutter. Place 2 inches apart on ungreased baking sheet.

3. Sprinkle cookies with cinnamon-sugar mixture. Bake at 375°F for 6 to 8 minutes or until edges are light golden brown. Cool 1 minute on baking sheet. Remove to cooling rack. Cool completely. Store in airtight container.

Makes 3 to 3½ dozen cookies

210

Tip: You can use your favorite cookie cutter in place of the star cookie cutter.

Mini Pizza Cookies

1 (18-ounce) tube refrigerated sugar cookie dough
2 cups (16 ounces) prepared pink frosting
  "M&M's"® Chocolate Mini Baking Bits
  Variety of additional toppings such as shredded coconut, granola, raisins, nuts, small pretzels, snack mixes, sunflower seeds, popped corn and mini marshmallows

Preheat oven to 350°F. Lightly grease cookie sheets; set aside. Divide dough into 8 equal portions. On lightly floured surface, roll each portion of dough into ¼-inch-thick circle; place about 2 inches apart onto prepared cookie sheets. Bake 10 to 13 minutes or until golden brown on edges. Cool completely on wire racks. Spread top of each pizza with frosting; sprinkle with "M&M's"® Chocolate Mini Baking Bits and 2 or 3 suggested toppings.

Makes 8 cookies

Cinnamon Stars

Worm Cookies

1¾ cups all-purpose flour
¾ cup powdered sugar
¼ cup unsweetened cocoa powder
⅛ teaspoon salt
1 cup butter
1 teaspoon vanilla
1 tube white frosting

1. Combine flour, sugar, cocoa and salt; set aside. Combine butter and vanilla in large bowl. Beat with electric mixer at medium-low speed until fluffy. Gradually beat in flour mixture until well combined. Cover and chill dough at least 30 minutes before rolling.

2. Preheat oven to 350°F. Form dough into 1½-inch balls. Roll balls gently with hands to form 5- to 6-inch logs about ½ inch thick. Shape into worms 2 inches apart on ungreased cookie sheets.

3. Bake 12 minutes or until set. Let stand on cookie sheets until cooled completely. Create eyes and stripes with white frosting.

Makes about 3 dozen cookies

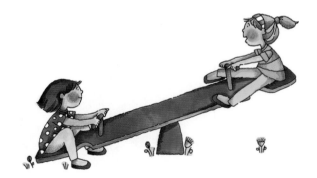

Cookie Clocks

1 package (18 ounces) refrigerated cookie dough, any flavor
All-purpose flour (optional)
Colored and white frostings and assorted candies

1. Preheat oven to 350°F. Grease cookie sheets.

2. Remove dough from wrapper according to package directions. Cut dough into 4 equal sections. Reserve 1 section; refrigerate remaining 3 sections. Sprinkle reserved dough with flour to minimize sticking, if necessary. Roll dough to ¼-inch thickness.

3. Cut out various shapes of clocks and watches as shown in photo. Carefully place cookies 2 inches apart on prepared cookie sheets. Repeat steps with remaining dough.

4. Bake 8 to 10 minutes or until edges are lightly browned. Cool cookies on cookie sheets 5 minutes. Remove to wire racks; cool completely. Decorate as desired.

Makes about 8 to 10 cookies

Fruity Cookie Rings and Twists

1 package (18 ounces) refrigerated sugar cookie dough
3 cups fruit-flavored cereal, crushed, divided

1. Remove dough from wrapper according to package directions. Combine dough and ½ cup crushed cereal in large bowl. Divide dough into 32 balls. Refrigerate 1 hour.

2. Preheat oven to 375°F. Shape dough balls into 6- to 8-inch-long ropes. Roll ropes in remaining cereal to coat; shape into rings or fold in half and twist.

3. Place cookies 2 inches apart on ungreased cookie sheets.

4. Bake 10 to 11 minutes or until lightly browned. Remove to wire racks; cool completely.

Makes 32 cookies

Tip: These cookie rings can be transformed into Christmas tree ornaments by poking a hole in each unbaked ring using a drinking straw. Bake cookies and decorate with colored gels and small candies to resemble wreaths. Loop thin ribbon through holes and tie ends together.

Super Chocolate Cookies

    2 cups all-purpose flour
    ⅓ cup unsweetened cocoa powder
    1 teaspoon baking soda
    ½ teaspoon salt
    1⅓ cups packed brown sugar
    ½ cup butter, softened
    ½ cup shortening
    2 eggs
    2 teaspoons vanilla
    1 cup candy-coated chocolate pieces
    1 cup raisins
    ¾ cup salted peanuts, coarsely chopped

1. Preheat oven to 350°F. Combine flour, cocoa, baking soda and salt in medium bowl; set aside.

2. Beat brown sugar, butter and shortening in large bowl of electric mixer at medium speed until light and fluffy. Beat in eggs and vanilla until well blended. Gradually add flour mixture, beating at low speed until blended. Stir in candy pieces, raisins and peanuts.

3. Drop dough by ¼ cupfuls onto ungreased cookie sheets, spacing 3 inches apart. Flatten slightly with fingertips. Bake cookies 13 to 15 minutes or until almost set. Cool 2 minutes on cookie sheets. Transfer to wire racks. Cool completely.   *Makes about 20 (4-inch) cookies*

Super Chocolate Cookies

Pretty Posies

1 package (18 ounces) refrigerated sugar cookie dough
Orange and purple food colorings
1 tablespoon sprinkles
All-purpose flour (optional)

1. Remove dough from wrapper. Reserve ⅙ of dough. Add orange food coloring and sprinkles to reserved dough until well blended; shape into 7½-inch log. Wrap with plastic wrap and refrigerate 30 minutes or until firm. Add purple food coloring to remaining dough until well blended. Shape dough into disc. Wrap with plastic wrap and refrigerate 30 minutes or until firm.

2. Roll out purple dough to 7½×6-inch rectangle on sheet of waxed paper. Place orange log in center of rectangle. Bring waxed paper and edges of purple dough up and over top of orange log; press gently. Overlap purple dough edges slightly; press gently. Wrap waxed paper around dough and twist ends to secure. Freeze log 20 minutes.

3. Preheat oven to 350°F. Lightly grease cookie sheets. Remove waxed paper from dough log; cut into ¼-inch slices. Place 2 inches apart on prepared cookie sheets. Using 2½-inch flower-shaped cookie cutter, cut slices into flowers; remove and discard dough scraps.

4. Bake 15 to 17 minutes or until edges are lightly browned. Remove to wire racks; cool completely.

Makes about 1½ dozen cookies

Peanut Butter Pizza Cookies

1¼ cups firmly packed light brown sugar
¾ cup JIF® Creamy Peanut Butter
½ CRISCO® Stick or ½ cup CRISCO® all-vegetable shortening
3 tablespoons milk
1 tablespoon vanilla
1 egg
1¾ cups all-purpose flour
¾ teaspoon salt
¾ teaspoon baking soda
8 ounces white baking chocolate, chopped
   Decorative candies

1. Heat oven to 375°F. Place sheets of foil on countertop for cooling cookies.

2. Combine brown sugar, peanut butter, ½ cup shortening, milk and vanilla in large bowl. Beat at medium speed of electric mixer until well blended. Add egg. Beat just until blended.

3. Combine flour, salt and baking soda. Add to creamed mixture at low speed. Mix just until blended.

4. Divide dough in half. Form each half into a ball. Place 1 ball of dough onto center of ungreased pizza pan or baking sheet. Spread dough with fingers to form a 12-inch circle. Repeat with remaining ball of dough.

5. Bake one baking sheet at a time at 375°F for 10 to 12 minutes, or until lightly browned. *Do not overbake.* Cool 2 minutes on baking sheet. Remove with large spatula to foil to cool completely.

6. Place white chocolate in a shallow microwave-safe bowl. Microwave on 100% (HIGH) for 30 seconds. Stir. Repeat at 30-second intervals until white chocolate is melted.

7. Spread melted white chocolate on center of cooled cookies to within ½ inch of edge. Decorate with candies. Let set completely. Cut into wedges.

Makes 2 pizzas

220

Handprints

1 package (18 ounces) refrigerated cookie dough, any flavor
All-purpose flour (optional)
Cookie glazes, frostings and assorted candies

1. Grease cookie sheets. Remove dough from wrapper according to package directions.

2. Cut dough into 4 equal sections. Reserve 1 section; refrigerate remaining 3 sections. Sprinkle reserved dough with flour to minimize sticking, if necessary.

3. Roll dough on prepared cookie sheet to 5×7-inch rectangle.

4. Place hand, palm-side down, on dough. Carefully, cut around outline of hand with knife. Remove scraps. Separate fingers as much as possible using small spatula. Pat fingers outward to lengthen slightly. Repeat steps with remaining dough.

5. Freeze dough 15 minutes. Preheat oven to 350°F.

6. Bake 7 to 13 minutes or until cookies are set and edges are golden brown. Cool completely on cookie sheets.

7. Decorate as desired.

Makes 4 adult handprint cookies

Tip: To get the kids involved, let them use their hands to make the handprints. Be sure that an adult is available to cut around the outline with a knife. The kids will enjoy seeing how their handprints bake into big cookies.

Sour Spirals

1 package (18 ounces) refrigerated sugar cookie dough
2 tablespoons plus 1½ teaspoons blue raspberry-flavored gelatin
¼ teaspoon gel blue food coloring
2 tablespoons plus 1½ teaspoons strawberry-flavored gelatin
¼ teaspoon gel red food coloring
  All-purpose flour

1. Remove dough from wrapper; divide in half. Reserve 1 dough half. Place remaining dough half in large bowl. Let dough stand about 10 minutes. Add blue raspberry-flavored gelatin and blue food coloring to dough in bowl; beat at medium speed of electric mixer until well blended and evenly colored. Wrap dough in plastic wrap; refrigerate 1 hour.

2. Combine reserved dough half, strawberry-flavored gelatin and red food coloring in large bowl. Beat at medium speed of electric mixer until well blended and evenly colored. Wrap dough in plastic wrap; refrigerate 1 hour.

3. Roll blue dough to 10×6-inch rectangle on lightly floured waxed paper using lightly floured rolling pin. Repeat with red dough. Refrigerate both dough rectangles 10 minutes.

4. Place blue dough rectangle over red dough. Remove waxed paper from blue dough. Starting at 10-inch side, roll up jelly-roll fashion into tight log. Wrap in plastic wrap; freeze 30 minutes.

5. Preheat oven to 350°F. Grease cookie sheets. Cut log into ¼-inch slices. Place on prepared cookie sheets. Bake 8 to 10 minutes or until cookies are firm. (Do not let cookies brown.) Cool on cookie sheets 2 to 3 minutes. Remove to wire racks; cool completely.

Makes about 2½ dozen cookies

Double Chocolate Sandwich Cookies

1 package (18 ounces) refrigerated sugar cookie dough
1 (3½- to 4-ounce) bar bittersweet chocolate candy, chopped
2 teaspoons butter
¾ cup milk chocolate chips

1. Preheat oven to 350°F.

2. Cut well-chilled cookie dough into ¼-inch-thick slices. Arrange slices 2 inches apart on ungreased cookie sheets. Cut 1-inch circles out of center of half of cookies.

3. Bake cookies 10 to 12 minutes or until edges are golden brown. Let stand on cookie sheets 2 minutes; transfer to wire racks. Cool completely.

4. Place bittersweet chocolate and butter in small heavy saucepan. Heat over low heat, stirring frequently, until chocolate is melted. Spread chocolate over bottoms of cookies without holes. Immediately top each chocolate-coated cookie with cookie with hole.

5. Place milk chocolate chips in small resealable plastic food storage bag; seal bag. Microwave at MEDIUM (50%) 1½ minutes. Turn bag over; microwave 1 to 1½ minutes or until melted. Knead bag until chocolate is smooth.

6. Cut very tiny corner off bag; drizzle chocolate decoratively over sandwich cookies. Let stand until chocolate is set, about 30 minutes. *Makes 16 sandwich cookies*

Tip: To cut 1-inch circles from the center of these cookies, use the wide end of a pastry bag tip, the removable center of a doughnut cutter or a melon baller.

Double Chocolate Sandwich Cookies

Cookie Cups

1 package (18 ounces) refrigerated sugar cookie dough
  All-purpose flour (optional)
  Prepared pudding, nondairy whipped topping, maraschino cherries, jelly beans, assorted sprinkles and small candies

1. Grease 12 (2¾-inch) muffin cups.

2. Remove dough from wrapper according to package directions. Sprinkle dough with flour to minimize sticking, if necessary.

3. Cut dough into 12 equal pieces; roll into balls. Place 1 ball in bottom of each muffin cup. Press dough halfway up sides of muffin cups, making indentation in centers.

4. Freeze muffin cups 15 minutes. Preheat oven to 350°F.

5. Bake 15 to 17 minutes or until golden brown. Cookies will be puffy. Remove from oven; gently press indentations with teaspoon.

6. Return to oven 1 to 2 minutes. Cool cookies in muffin cups 5 minutes. Remove to wire rack; cool completely.

7. Fill each cookie cup with desired fillings. Decorate as desired. *Makes 12 cookies*

Giant Cookie Cups Variation: Grease 10 (3¾-inch) muffin cups. Cut dough into 10 pieces; roll into balls. Complete recipe according to regular Cookie Cups directions. Makes 10 giant cookie cups.

Tip: Add some pizzazz to your cookie cups by filling with a mixture of prepared fruit-flavored gelatin combined with prepared pudding or nondairy whipped topping. For convenience, snack-size gelatins and puddings can be found at the supermarket, so there is no need to make them from scratch.

228

Peanut Butter and Jelly Pinwheels

1 Butter Flavor CRISCO® Stick or 1 cup Butter Flavor CRISCO® All-Vegetable Shortening
1 cup JIF® Creamy Peanut Butter
¾ cup granulated sugar
¾ cup firmly packed light brown sugar
2 eggs
1 teaspoon vanilla
2½ cups all-purpose flour
1 teaspoon salt
1 teaspoon baking soda
½ cup SMUCKER'S® Seedless Red Raspberry Jam*
⅔ cup very finely chopped peanuts

*If desired, top with additional jam before serving.

Combine 1 cup shortening, peanut butter, granulated sugar and brown sugar in large bowl. Beat at medium speed of electric mixer until well blended. Beat in eggs and vanilla.

Combine flour, salt and baking soda. Add gradually to creamed mixture at low speed. Beat until well blended.

Cut parchment paper to line 17×11-inch pan. Press dough out to edges of paper. Spread with jam to within ½ inch of edges.

Lift up long side of paper. Loosen dough with spatula. Roll up dough jelly-roll fashion; seal seam. Sprinkle nuts on paper; roll dough over nuts. Press any remaining nuts into dough. Wrap rolled-up dough in parchment paper; place in plastic bag. Refrigerate overnight.

Preheat oven to 375°F.

Line baking sheet with foil or parchment paper. Unwrap dough and cut into ½-inch slices. Place 2 inches apart on prepared baking sheet.

Bake for 10 to 12 minutes or until set. Cool about 5 minutes on baking sheet before removing to new foil to cool completely.

Makes 3 dozen cookies

Lollipop Clowns

1 package (18 ounces) refrigerated red, green or blue cookie dough*
All-purpose flour (optional)
Assorted colored icings and hard candies

SUPPLIES
18 (4-inch) lollipop sticks

*If colored dough is unavailable, sugar cookie dough can be tinted with paste food coloring.

1. Preheat oven to 350°F.

2. Remove dough from wrapper according to package directions. Divide dough into 2 equal sections. Reserve 1 section; cover and refrigerate remaining section.

3. Roll reserved dough on lightly floured surface to 1/8-inch thickness. Sprinkle with flour to minimize sticking, if necessary.

4. Cut out cookies using 3½-inch round cookie cutter. Place lollipop sticks on cookies so that tips of sticks are imbedded in cookies. Carefully turn cookies so sticks are in back; place on ungreased cookie sheets. Repeat with remaining dough.

5. Bake 8 to 10 minutes or until firm but not brown. Cool on cookie sheets 2 minutes. Remove to wire racks; cool completely.

6. Decorate cookies with icings as shown in photo.   *Makes about 18 cookies*

Tip: These happy clown faces make the perfect topping for a birthday cake. Stick a Lollipop Clown, one for each child, in the cake for a wonderful circus theme party.

232

Peanut Butter and Chocolate Spirals

1 package (18 ounces) refrigerated sugar cookie dough
1 package (18 ounces) refrigerated peanut butter cookie dough
¼ cup unsweetened cocoa powder
⅓ cup peanut butter-flavored chips, chopped
¼ cup all-purpose flour
⅓ cup miniature chocolate chips

1. Remove each dough from wrapper according to package directions.

2. Place sugar cookie dough and cocoa in large bowl; mix until well blended. Stir in peanut butter chips.

3. Place peanut butter cookie dough and flour in another large bowl; mix until well blended. Stir in chocolate chips. Divide each dough in half; cover and refrigerate 1 hour.

4. Roll each dough on floured surface to 12×6-inch rectangle. Layer each half of peanut butter dough onto each half of chocolate dough. Roll up doughs, starting at long end to form 2 (12-inch) rolls. Wrap in plastic wrap; refrigerate 1 hour.

5. Preheat oven to 375°F. Cut dough into ½-inch-thick slices. Place cookies 2 inches apart on ungreased cookie sheets.

6. Bake 10 to 12 minutes or until lightly browned. Remove to wire racks; cool completely.

Makes 4 dozen cookies

Peanut Butter and Chocolate Spirals

Cookie Sundae Cups

1 package (18 ounces) refrigerated chocolate chip cookie dough
6 cups ice cream, any flavor
1¼ cups ice cream topping, any flavor
Whipped cream
Colored sprinkles

1. Preheat oven to 350°F. Line 18 (2½-inch) muffin pan cups with paper baking cups.

2. Remove dough from wrapper. Divide dough into 18 equal pieces; shape into balls. Place 1 dough ball in each prepared muffin cup; press dough onto bottoms and up sides of muffin cups.

3. Bake 14 to 18 minutes or until golden brown. Cool in muffin cups 10 minutes. Remove to wire rack; cool completely.

4. Place ⅓ cup ice cream in each cookie cup. Drizzle with ice cream topping. Top with whipped cream and colored sprinkles. *Makes 1½ dozen desserts*

236

Chocolate Peanut Butter Cookies

1 package DUNCAN HINES® Moist Deluxe® Devil's Food Cake Mix
¾ cup crunchy peanut butter
2 eggs
2 tablespoons milk
1 cup candy-coated peanut butter pieces

1. Preheat oven to 350°F. Grease baking sheets.

2. Combine cake mix, peanut butter, eggs and milk in large mixing bowl. Beat at low speed with electric mixer until blended. Stir in peanut butter pieces.

3. Drop dough by slightly rounded tablespoonfuls onto prepared baking sheets. Bake 7 to 9 minutes or until lightly browned. Cool 2 minutes on baking sheets. Remove to cooling racks. *Makes about 3½ dozen cookies*

Tip: You can use 1 cup peanut butter chips in place of peanut butter pieces.

Cookie Sundae Cup

Dino-Mite Dinosaurs

    1 cup (2 sticks) butter, softened
1¼ cups granulated sugar
    1 large egg
    2 squares (1 ounce each) semi-sweet chocolate, melted
    ½ teaspoon vanilla extract
2⅓ cups all-purpose flour
    1 teaspoon baking powder
    ¼ teaspoon salt
    1 cup white frosting
       Assorted food colorings
    1 cup "M&M's"® Chocolate Mini Baking Bits

In large bowl cream butter and sugar until light and fluffy; beat in egg, chocolate and vanilla. In medium bowl combine flour, baking powder and salt; add to creamed mixture. Wrap and refrigerate dough 2 to 3 hours. Preheat oven to 350°F. Working with half the dough at a time on lightly floured surface, roll to ¼-inch thickness. Cut into dinosaur shapes using 4-inch cookie cutters. Place about 2 inches apart on ungreased cookie sheets. Bake 10 to 12 minutes. Cool 2 minutes on cookie sheets; cool completely on wire racks. Tint frosting desired colors. Frost cookies and decorate with "M&M's"® Chocolate Mini Baking Bits. Store in tightly covered container.

Makes 2 dozen cookies

238

Peanut Butter and Jelly Sandwich Cookies

1 package (18 ounces) refrigerated sugar cookie dough
1 tablespoon unsweetened cocoa powder
　All-purpose flour (optional)
¾ cup creamy peanut butter
½ cup grape jam or jelly

1. Remove dough from wrapper according to package directions. Reserve ¼ section of dough; cover and refrigerate remaining ¾ section of dough. Combine reserved dough and cocoa in small bowl; cover and refrigerate.

2. Shape remaining ¾ section of dough into 5½-inch log. Sprinkle with flour to minimize sticking, if necessary. Remove chocolate dough from refrigerator; roll on sheet of waxed paper to 9½×6½-inch rectangle. Place dough log in center of rectangle.

3. Bring waxed paper edges and chocolate dough up and together over log. Press gently on top and sides of dough so entire log is wrapped in chocolate dough. Flatten log slightly to form square. Wrap in waxed paper. Freeze 10 minutes.

4. Preheat oven to 350°F. Remove waxed paper. Cut dough into ¼-inch slices. Place slices 2 inches apart on ungreased cookie sheets. Reshape dough edges into square, if necessary. Press dough slightly to form indentation so dough resembles slice of bread.

5. Bake 8 to 11 minutes or until lightly browned. Remove from oven and straighten cookie edges with spatula. Cool 2 minutes on cookie sheets. Remove to wire racks; cool completely.

6. To make sandwich, spread about 1 tablespoon peanut butter on bottom of 1 cookie. Spread about ½ tablespoon jam over peanut butter; top with second cookie, pressing gently. Repeat with remaining cookies. *Makes 11 sandwich cookies*

Tip: Cut each sandwich diagonally in half for a smaller cookie and fun look.

240

Cookie Pops

    1 package (18 ounces) refrigerated sugar cookie dough
       All-purpose flour (optional)
  20 (4-inch) lollipop sticks
       Assorted frostings, glazes and decors

1. Preheat oven to 350°F. Grease cookie sheets. Remove dough from wrapper according to package directions. Sprinkle with flour to minimize sticking, if necessary.

2. Cut dough in half. Reserve 1 half; refrigerate remaining dough. Roll reserved dough to ⅛-inch thickness. Cut out cookies using 3½-inch cookie cutters.

3. Place lollipop sticks on cookies so that tips of sticks are imbedded in cookies. Carefully turn cookies so sticks are in back; place on prepared cookie sheets. Repeat with remaining dough.

4. Bake 7 to 11 minutes or until edges are lightly browned. Cool cookies on cookie sheets 2 minutes. Remove cookies to wire racks; cool completely. Decorate with frostings, glazes and decors as desired.

Makes 20 cookies

242

Beautiful Butterflies

    1 package (18 ounces) refrigerated sugar cookie dough
  24 wooden craft sticks
    6 squares (1 ounce each) white chocolate
       Assorted food colorings
    1 cup "M&M's"® Chocolate Mini Baking Bits

Preheat oven to 325°F. Working with half the dough at a time on lightly floured surface, roll to ¼-inch thickness. Cut into butterfly shapes using 3-inch cookie cutters. Press on craft sticks and place about 2 inches apart on ungreased cookie sheets. Bake 10 to 12 minutes. Cool 2 minutes on cookie sheets; cool completely on wire racks. In top of double boiler over hot water melt white chocolate. Remove from heat; divide among separate bowls for each glaze color desired. Tint with food colorings as desired. Spread colored white chocolate over cookies; decorate with "M&M's"® Chocolate Mini Baking Bits. Let set. Store in tightly covered container.

Makes 2 dozen cookies

Smushy Cookies

1 package (18 ounces) refrigerated cookie dough, any flavor
All-purpose flour (optional)

FILLINGS
Peanut butter, multi-colored miniature marshmallows, assorted colored sprinkles, chocolate-covered raisins and caramel candy squares

1. Preheat oven to 350°F. Grease cookie sheets.

2. Remove dough from wrapper according to package directions. Cut into 4 equal sections. Reserve 1 section; refrigerate remaining 3 sections.

3. Roll reserved dough to ¼-inch thickness. Sprinkle with flour to minimize sticking, if necessary. Cut out cookies using 2½-inch round cookie cutter. Transfer to prepared cookie sheets. Repeat with remaining dough, working with 1 section at a time.

4. Bake 8 to 11 minutes or until edges are light golden brown. Remove to wire racks; cool completely.

5. To make sandwich, spread about 1½ tablespoons peanut butter on bottom of 1 cookie to within ¼ inch of edge. Sprinkle with miniature marshmallows, sprinkles and candy pieces. Top with second cookie, pressing gently. Repeat with remaining cookies and fillings.

6. Just before serving, place sandwiches on paper towels. Microwave at HIGH 15 to 25 seconds or until fillings become soft.   *Makes about 8 to 10 sandwich cookies*

Tip: Invite the neighbor kids over on a rainy day to make these fun Smushy Cookies. Be sure to have lots of filling choices available so each child can create their own unique cookies.

244

Peanut Butter Bears

    2 cups uncooked quick-cooking oats
    2 cups all-purpose flour
    1 tablespoon baking powder
    1 cup granulated sugar
    ¾ cup butter, softened
    ½ cup creamy peanut butter
    ½ cup packed brown sugar
    ½ cup cholesterol-free egg substitute
    1 teaspoon vanilla
    3 tablespoons miniature chocolate chips

1. Stir together oats, flour and baking powder; set aside.

2. Beat granulated sugar, butter, peanut butter and brown sugar in large bowl with mixer at medium-high speed until creamy. Add egg substitute and vanilla; beat until light and fluffy. Add oat mixture. Beat on low speed until combined. Cover and refrigerate 1 to 2 hours or until firm.

3. Preheat oven to 375°F.

4. For each bear, shape one 1-inch ball for body and one ¾-inch ball for head. Place body and head together on baking sheet; flatten slightly. Make 7 small balls for ears, arms, legs and mouth. Place on bear body and head. Place 2 chocolate chips on each head for eyes; place 1 chocolate chip on each body for belly-button.

5. Bake 9 to 11 minutes or until light brown. Cool 1 minute on cookie sheet. Remove to wire racks; cool completely.

Makes 4 dozen cookies

Peanut Butter Bear

Colorful Cookie Buttons

1½ cups (3 sticks) butter, softened
½ cup granulated sugar
½ cup firmly packed light brown sugar
2 large egg yolks
1 teaspoon vanilla extract
3½ cups all-purpose flour
1½ teaspoons baking powder
½ teaspoon salt
1 cup "M&M's"® Chocolate Mini Baking Bits

Preheat oven to 350°F. In large bowl cream butter and sugars until light and fluffy; beat in egg yolks and vanilla. In medium bowl combine flour, baking powder and salt; add to creamed mixture. Shape dough into 72 balls. For each cookie, place one ball on ungreased cookie sheet and flatten. Place 8 to 10 "M&M's"® Chocolate Mini Baking Bits on dough. Flatten second ball and place over "M&M's"® Chocolate Mini Baking Bits, pressing top and bottom dough together. Decorate top with remaining "M&M's"® Chocolate Mini Baking Bits. Repeat with remaining dough balls and "M&M's"® Chocolate Mini Baking Bits, placing cookies about 2 inches apart on cookie sheet. Bake 17 to 18 minutes. Cool 2 minutes on cookie sheets; cool completely on wire racks. Store in tightly covered container.   *Makes 3 dozen cookies*

248

Kitty Cookies

1 package (18 ounces) refrigerated sugar cookie dough or desired flavor
All-purpose flour (optional)
White Decorator Frosting (recipe follows)
Assorted food colorings
Assorted colored candies and red licorice

1. Preheat oven to 350°F. Remove dough from wrapper according to package directions. Divide dough in half. Reserve 1 half; cover and refrigerate remaining half.

2. Roll reserved dough on lightly floured surface to ⅛-inch thickness. Sprinkle with flour to minimize sticking, if necessary. Cut out dough using 3½-inch kitty face cookie cutter. Place cutouts 2 inches apart on ungreased baking sheets. Repeat with remaining dough and scraps.

3. Bake 8 to 10 minutes or until firm but not browned. Cool on baking sheets 2 minutes. Remove to wire racks; cool completely.

4. Prepare White Decorator Frosting. Tint with food colorings as desired. Decorate cookies with frosting and assorted candies to create kitty faces, using licorice for whiskers.

Makes about 20 cookies

White Decorator Frosting

4 cups powdered sugar
½ cup vegetable shortening or unsalted butter
1 tablespoon corn syrup
6 to 8 tablespoons milk

Beat sugar, shortening, corn syrup and milk in medium bowl at high speed of electric mixer 2 minutes or until fluffy.

Peanut Butter and Jelly Cookies

1 Butter Flavor CRISCO® Stick or 1 cup Butter Flavor CRISCO® all-vegetable shortening
1 cup JIF® Creamy Peanut Butter
1 teaspoon vanilla
⅔ cup firmly packed light brown sugar
⅓ cup granulated sugar
2 large eggs
2 cups all-purpose flour
1 cup SMUCKER'S® Strawberry Preserves or any flavor

1. Heat oven to 350°F.

2. Combine 1 cup shortening, peanut butter and vanilla in food processor fitted with metal blade. Process until well blended and smooth. Add sugars; process until incorporated completely. Add eggs; beat just until blended. Add flour; pulse until dough begins to form ball. *Do not overprocess.*

3. Place dough in medium bowl. Shape ½ tablespoon dough into ball for each cookie. Place 1½ inches apart on ungreased cookie sheets. Press thumb into center of each ball to create deep well. Fill each well with about ½ teaspoon preserves.

4. Bake at 350°F for 10 minutes or until lightly browned and firm. Cool on cookie sheets 4 minutes; transfer to cooling racks. Leave on racks about 30 minutes or until completely cool.

Makes about 5 dozen cookies

252

Snowmen

1 package (18 ounces) refrigerated chocolate chip cookie dough
1½ cups sifted powdered sugar
2 tablespoons milk
   Candy corn, gumdrops, chocolate chips, licorice and other assorted small candies

1. Preheat oven to 375°F. Remove dough from wrapper. Cut dough into 12 equal sections. Divide each section into 3 balls: large, medium and small for each snowman.

2. For each snowman, place 3 balls in row, ¼ inch apart, on ungreased cookie sheet.

3. Bake 10 to 12 minutes or until edges are very lightly browned. Cool 4 minutes on cookie sheets. Remove to wire racks; cool completely.

4. Mix powdered sugar and milk in medium bowl until smooth. Pour over cookies. Let cookies stand 20 minutes or until set.

5. Decorate with assorted candies to create snowman faces, hats and arms.

Makes 1 dozen cookies

254

Captivating Caterpillar Cupcakes

> 1 package DUNCAN HINES® Moist Deluxe® White Cake Mix
> 3 egg whites
> 1⅓ cups water
> 2 tablespoons vegetable oil
> ½ cup star decors, divided
> 1 container DUNCAN HINES® Vanilla Frosting
> Green food coloring
> 6 chocolate sandwich cookies, finely crushed (see Tip)
> ½ cup candy-coated chocolate pieces
> ⅓ cup assorted jelly beans
> Assorted nonpareil decors

1. Preheat oven to 350°F. Place 24 (2½-inch) paper liners in muffin cups.

2. Combine cake mix, egg whites, water and oil in large bowl. Beat at low speed with electric mixer until moistened. Beat at medium speed 2 minutes. Fold in ⅓ cup star decors. Fill paper liners about half full. Bake at 350°F for 18 to 23 minutes or until toothpick inserted in center comes out clean. Cool in pans 5 minutes. Remove to cooling racks. Cool completely.

3. Tint vanilla frosting with green food coloring. Frost one cupcake. Sprinkle ½ teaspoon chocolate cookie crumbs on frosting. Arrange 4 candy-coated chocolate pieces to form caterpillar body. Place jelly bean at one end to form head. Attach remaining star and nonpareil decors with dots of frosting to form eyes. Repeat with remaining cupcakes.

Makes 24 cupcakes

Tip: To finely crush chocolate sandwich cookies, place cookies in resealable plastic bag. Remove excess air from bag; seal. Press rolling pin on top of cookies to break into pieces. Continue pressing until evenly crushed.

Captivating Caterpillar Cupcakes

Play Ball

  2 cups plus 1 tablespoon all-purpose flour, divided
  ¾ cup granulated sugar
  ¾ cup packed brown sugar
  1 tablespoon baking powder
  1 teaspoon salt
  ½ teaspoon baking soda
1¼ cups milk
  3 eggs
  ½ cup shortening
1½ teaspoons vanilla
  ½ cup mini semisweet chocolate chips
  1 container (16 ounces) vanilla frosting
    Assorted candies and food colorings

1. Preheat oven to 350°F. Line 24 regular-size (2½-inch) muffin pan cups with paper baking cups.

2. Combine 2 cups flour, sugars, baking powder, salt and baking soda in medium bowl. Beat milk, eggs, shortening and vanilla in large bowl with electric mixer at medium speed until well combined. Add flour mixture; blend well. Beat at high speed 3 minutes, scraping side of bowl frequently. Toss mini chocolate chips with remaining 1 tablespoon flour; stir into batter. Divide evenly among prepared muffin cups.

3. Bake 20 minutes or until toothpick inserted into centers comes out clean. Cool in pan on wire racks 5 minutes. Remove cupcakes to racks; cool completely. Decorate with desired frostings and candies as shown in photo.

Makes 24 cupcakes

Mini Turtle Cupcakes

1 package (21.5 ounces) brownie mix plus ingredients to prepare mix
½ cup chopped pecans
1 cup prepared or homemade dark chocolate frosting
½ cup chopped pecans, toasted
12 caramels, unwrapped
1 to 2 tablespoons whipping cream

1. Heat oven to 350°F. Line 54 mini (1½-inch) muffin cups with paper baking cups.

2. Prepare brownie batter as directed on package. Stir in chopped pecans.

3. Spoon batter into prepared muffin cups filling ⅔ full. Bake 18 minutes or until toothpick inserted into centers comes out clean. Cool in pans on wire racks 5 minutes. Remove cupcakes to racks; cool completely. (At this point, cupcakes may be frozen up to 3 months. Thaw at room temperature before frosting.)

4. Spread frosting over cooled cupcakes; top with pecans.

5. Combine caramels and 1 tablespoon cream in small saucepan. Cook over low heat until caramels are melted and mixture is smooth, stirring constantly. Add additional 1 tablespoon cream if needed. Drizzle caramel decoratively over cupcakes. Store at room temperature up to 24 hours or cover and refrigerate up to 3 days.

Makes 54 mini cupcakes

260

Porcupine Cupcakes

1 package DUNCAN HINES® Moist Deluxe® Cake Mix (any flavor)
1 container DUNCAN HINES® Chocolate Frosting
Sliced almonds

1. Preheat oven to 350°F. Place 2½-inch paper liners in 24 muffin cups.

2. Prepare, bake and cool cupcakes following package directions for basic recipe. Frost cupcakes with Chocolate frosting. Place sliced almonds upright on each cupcake to decorate as a "porcupine."

Makes 24 cupcakes

Tip: Slivered almonds can be used in place of sliced almonds.

Snowman Cupcakes

1 package (about 18 ounces) yellow or white cake mix, plus ingredients to prepare mix
2 containers (16 ounces each) vanilla frosting
4 cups flaked coconut
15 large marshmallows
15 miniature chocolate covered peanut butter cups, unwrapped
Small red candies and pretzel sticks for decoration
Green and red decorating gel

Preheat oven to 350°F. Line 15 regular-size (2½-inch) muffin pan cups and 15 small (about 1-inch) muffin pan cups with paper baking cups. Prepare cake mix according to package directions. Spoon batter into prepared muffin cups.

Bake 15 to 20 minutes for large cupcakes and 10 to 15 minutes for small cupcakes or until cupcakes are golden and toothpick inserted into centers comes out clean. Cool in pans on wire racks 10 minutes. Remove from pans to racks; cool completely. Remove paper baking cups.

For each snowman, frost bottom and side of 1 large cupcake; coat with coconut. Repeat with 1 small cupcake. Attach small cupcake to large cupcake with frosting to form snowman body. Attach marshmallow to small cupcake with frosting to form snowman head. Attach inverted peanut butter cup to marshmallow with frosting to form snowman hat. Use pretzels for arms and small red candies for buttons as shown in photo. Pipe faces with decorating gel as shown. Repeat with remaining cupcakes.

Makes 15 snowmen

262

Snowman Cupcakes

Red's Rockin' Rainbow Cupcakes

2¼ cups all-purpose flour
1 tablespoon baking powder
½ teaspoon salt
1⅔ cups granulated sugar
½ cup (1 stick) butter, softened
1 cup milk
2 teaspoons vanilla extract
3 large egg whites
Blue and assorted food colorings
1 container (16 ounces) white frosting
1½ cups "M&M's"® Chocolate Mini Baking Bits, divided

Preheat oven to 350°F. Lightly grease 24 (2¾-inch) muffin cups or line with paper or foil liners; set aside. In large bowl combine flour, baking powder and salt. Blend in sugar, butter, milk and vanilla; beat about 2 minutes. Add egg whites; beat 2 minutes. Divide batter evenly among prepared muffin cups. Place 2 drops desired food coloring into each muffin cup. Swirl gently with knife. Sprinkle evenly with ¾ cup "M&M's"® Chocolate Mini Baking Bits. Bake 20 to 25 minutes or until toothpick inserted in center comes out clean. Cool completely on wire racks. Combine frosting and blue food coloring. Spread frosting over cupcakes; decorate with remaining ¾ cup "M&M's"® Chocolate Mini Baking Bits to make rainbows. Store in tightly covered container.

Makes 24 cupcakes

Red's Rockin' Rainbow Cupcakes

Lazy Daisy Cupcakes

    1 package (about 18 ounces) yellow cake mix, plus ingredients to prepare mix
      Food coloring
    1 container (16 ounces) vanilla frosting
   30 large marshmallows
   24 small round candies or gum drops

1. Line standard (2½-inch) muffin cups with paper liners or spray with nonstick cooking spray. Prepare cake mix and bake in muffin cups according to package directions. Cool in pans on wire racks 15 minutes. Remove cupcakes from pans and cool completely on wire racks.

2. Add food coloring to frosting, a few drops at a time, until desired color is reached. Frost cooled cupcakes with tinted frosting.

3. With scissors, cut each marshmallow crosswise into 4 pieces. Stretch pieces into petal shapes; place 5 pieces on each cupcake to form flower. Place candy in center of each flower.

Makes 24 cupcakes

Clown Cupcakes

    1 package DUNCAN HINES® Moist Deluxe® Classic Yellow Cake Mix
  12 scoops vanilla ice cream
  12 sugar ice cream cones
    1 container (7 ounces) refrigerated aerosol whipped cream
      Assorted colored decors and assorted candies for eyes, nose and mouth

1. Preheat oven to 350°F. Place 2½-inch paper liners in 24 muffin cups.

2. Prepare, bake and cool cupcakes following package directions.

3. Remove paper from 12 cupcakes. Place top-side down on serving plates. Top with scoops of ice cream. Place cones on ice cream for hats. Spray whipped cream around bottom of cupcakes for collars. Spray three small dots up front on cones. Sprinkle whipped cream with assorted colored decors. Use candies to make clowns' faces.

Makes 12 clown cupcakes

Note: This recipe makes 24 cupcakes: 12 to make into "clowns" and 12 to freeze for later use.

Lazy Daisy Cupcake

Caramel Apple Cupcakes

1 package (about 18 ounces) butter-recipe yellow cake mix plus ingredients to prepare mix
1 cup chopped dried apples
  Caramel Frosting (recipe follows)
  Chopped nuts (optional)

1. Preheat oven to 375°F. Line 24 regular-size (2½-inch) muffin pan cups with paper baking cups.

2. Prepare cake mix according to package directions. Stir in apples. Spoon batter into prepared muffin cups.

3. Bake 15 to 20 minutes or until toothpick inserted into centers comes out clean. Cool in pans on wire racks 10 minutes. Remove to racks; cool completely.

4. Prepare Caramel Frosting. Frost cupcakes. Sprinkle cupcakes with nuts, if desired.

Makes 24 cupcakes

268

Caramel Frosting

 3 tablespoons butter
 1 cup packed brown sugar
 ½ cup evaporated milk
 ⅛ teaspoon salt
3¾ cups powdered sugar
 ¾ teaspoon vanilla

1. Melt butter in 2-quart saucepan. Stir in brown sugar, evaporated milk and salt. Bring to a boil, stirring constantly. Remove from heat; cool to lukewarm.

2. Beat in powdered sugar until frosting is of spreading consistency. Blend in vanilla.

Vanilla-Strawberry Cupcakes

CUPCAKES
- 2 cups all-purpose flour
- 2 teaspoons baking powder
- ¼ teaspoon salt
- 1¾ cups granulated sugar
- ½ cup (1 stick) butter, softened
- ¾ cup 2% or whole milk
- 1½ teaspoons vanilla
- 3 large egg whites
- ½ cup strawberry preserves

FROSTING
- 1 package (8 ounces) cream cheese (do not use fat-free), chilled, cut into cubes
- ¼ cup (½ stick) butter, softened
- 2 teaspoons vanilla
- 2 cups powdered sugar
- 1 to 1½ cups small fresh strawberry slices

270

1. Preheat oven to 350°F. Line 28 regular-size (2½-inch) muffin pan cups with paper baking cups.

2. For cupcakes, combine flour, baking powder and salt in medium bowl; mix well and set aside. Beat granulated sugar and butter with electric mixer at medium speed 1 minute. Add milk and vanilla. Beat at low speed 30 seconds. Gradually beat in flour mixture; beat at medium speed 2 minutes. Add egg whites; beat 1 minute.

3. Spoon batter into prepared muffin cups filling ½ full. Drop 1 teaspoon preserves on top of batter; swirl into batter with toothpick. Bake 20 to 22 minutes or until toothpick inserted into centers comes out clean. Cool in pans on wire racks 10 minutes. Remove cupcakes to racks; cool completely. (At this point, cupcakes may be frozen up to 3 months. Thaw at room temperature before frosting.)

4. For frosting, process cream cheese, butter and vanilla in food processor just until combined. Add powdered sugar; pulse just until sugar is incorporated. (Do not overmix or frosting will be too soft to spread).

5. Spread frosting over cooled cupcakes; decorate with sliced strawberries. Serve within 1 hour or refrigerate up to 8 hours before serving.

Makes 28 cupcakes

Ice Cream Cone Cupcakes

1 package (18¼ ounces) white cake mix plus ingredients to prepare mix
2 tablespoons nonpareils*
2 packages (1¾ ounces each) flat-bottomed ice cream cones (about 24 cones)
1 container (16 ounces) vanilla or chocolate frosting
Candies and other decorations

*Nonpareils are tiny, round, brightly colored sprinkles used for cake and cookie decorating.

1. Preheat oven to 350°F.

2. Prepare cake mix according to package directions. Stir in nonpareils.

3. Spoon ¼ cup batter into each ice cream cone.

4. Stand cones on cookie sheet. Bake cones until toothpick inserted into center of cupcake comes out clean, about 20 minutes. Cool on wire racks.

5. Frost each filled cone. Decorate as desired.

Makes 24 cupcakes

Note: Cupcakes are best served the day they are prepared. Store loosely covered.

Ice Cream Cone Cupcakes

Cubcakes

  1 package (about 18 ounces) chocolate cake mix, plus ingredients to prepare mix
  1 container (16 ounces) chocolate frosting
  1 package (5 ounces) chocolate nonpareils
 72 red cinnamon candies
    Chocolate sprinkles
  1 tube (0.6 ounce) black piping gel

1. Line standard (2½-inch) muffin cups with paper liners or spray with nonstick cooking spray. Prepare cake mix and bake in muffin cups according to package directions. Cool in pans on wire racks 15 minutes. Remove cupcakes from pans and cool completely.

2. Frost cooled cupcakes with chocolate frosting. Use nonpareils for ears and muzzle, red candies for eyes and nose and chocolate sprinkles for fur. Use piping gel to place dots on eyes and to create mouth.

Makes 24 cupcakes

274

Golden Apple Cupcakes

  1 package (18 to 20 ounces) yellow cake mix
  1 cup MOTT'S® Chunky Apple Sauce
 ⅓ cup vegetable oil
  3 eggs
 ¼ cup firmly packed light brown sugar
 ¼ cup chopped walnuts
 ½ teaspoon ground cinnamon
    Vanilla Frosting (recipe follows)

Heat oven to 350°F. In bowl, combine cake mix, apple sauce, oil and eggs; blend according to package directions. Spoon batter into 24 paper-lined muffin pan cups. Mix brown sugar, walnuts and cinnamon; sprinkle over prepared batter in muffin cups. Bake 20 to 25 minutes or until toothpick inserted in center comes out clean. Cool in pan 10 minutes. Remove from pan; cool completely on wire rack. Frost cupcakes with Vanilla Frosting.

Makes 24 cupcakes

Vanilla Frosting: Beat 1 package (8 ounces) softened cream cheese until creamy; blend in ¼ teaspoon vanilla. Beat ½ cup heavy cream until stiff; fold into cream cheese mixture.

Cubcakes

Pretty-in-Pink Peppermint Cupcakes

    1 package (about 18 ounces) white cake mix
1⅓ cups water
    3 large egg whites
    2 tablespoons vegetable oil or melted butter
    ½ teaspoon peppermint extract
    3 to 4 drops red liquid food coloring *or* ¼ teaspoon gel food coloring
    1 container (16 ounces) prepared vanilla frosting
    ½ cup crushed peppermint candies (about 16 candies)

1. Preheat oven to 350°F. Line 30 regular-size (2½-inch) muffin pan cups with pink or white paper baking cups.

2. Beat cake mix, water, egg whites, oil, peppermint extract and food coloring with electric mixer at low speed 30 seconds. Beat at medium speed 2 minutes.

3. Spoon batter into prepared muffin cups filling ¾ full. Bake 20 to 22 minutes or until toothpick inserted into centers comes out clean. Cool in pans on wire racks 10 minutes. Remove cupcakes to racks; cool completely. (At this point, cupcakes may be frozen up to 3 months. Thaw at room temperature before frosting.)

4. Spread cooled cupcakes with frosting; top with crushed candies. Store at room temperature up to 24 hours or cover and refrigerate up to 3 days before serving.

Makes about 30 cupcakes

276

Pretty-in-Pink Peppermint Cupcakes

Double Malted Cupcakes

CUPCAKES
- 2 cups all-purpose flour
- ¼ cup malted milk powder
- 2 teaspoons baking powder
- ¼ teaspoon salt
- 1¾ cups granulated sugar
- ½ cup (1 stick) butter, softened
- 1 cup 2% or whole milk
- 1½ teaspoons vanilla
- 3 large egg whites

FROSTING
- 4 ounces milk chocolate candy bar, broken into chunks
- ¼ cup (½ stick) butter
- ¼ cup whipping cream
- 1 tablespoon malted milk powder
- 1 teaspoon vanilla
- 1¾ cups powdered sugar
- 30 chocolate-covered malt ball candies

1. Preheat oven to 350°F. Line 30 regular-size (2½-inch) muffin cups with paper baking cups.

2. For cupcakes, combine flour, ¼ cup malted milk powder, baking powder and salt; mix well and set aside. Beat granulated sugar and ½ cup butter with electric mixer at medium speed 1 minute. Add milk and 1½ teaspoons vanilla. Beat at low speed 30 seconds. Gradually beat in flour mixture; beat at medium speed 2 minutes. Add egg whites; beat 1 minute.

3. Spoon batter into prepared muffin cups filling ⅔ full. Bake 20 minutes or until golden brown and toothpick inserted into centers comes out clean. Cool in pans on wire racks 10 minutes. (Centers of cupcakes will sink slightly upon cooling.) Remove cupcakes to racks; cool completely. (At this point, cupcakes may be frozen up to 3 months.)

4. For frosting, melt chocolate and ¼ cup butter in heavy saucepan over low heat, stirring frequently. Stir in cream, 1 tablespoon malted milk powder and 1 teaspoon vanilla; mix well. Gradually stir in powdered sugar. Cook and stir 4 to 5 minutes until small lumps disappear. Remove from heat. Chill 20 minutes, beating every 5 minutes until frosting is spreadable. Spread cooled cupcakes with frosting; decorate with chocolate-covered malt ball candies.

Makes 30 cupcakes

I Think You're "Marbleous" Cupcakes

   1 box (18½ ounces) pudding-in-the-mix cake mix, any flavor
1¼ cups water
   3 eggs
¼ cup oil
   1 container (16 ounces) vanilla frosting
   1 tube (4¼ ounces) red decorating icing

SUPPLIES
   Decorating tips to fit tube of icing

1. Preheat oven to 350°F. Grease or paper-line 24 (2½-inch) muffin cups.

2. Prepare cake mix according to package directions with water, eggs and oil. Spoon batter into prepared pans, filling each ⅔ full.

3. Bake 20 to 25 minutes or until toothpick inserted into centers comes out clean. Cool in pans 20 minutes. Remove to wire rack and cool completely.

4. Spread 1½ to 2 tablespoons frosting over each cupcake. Fit round tip onto tube of icing. Squeeze 4 to 5 dots icing over each cupcake. Swirl toothpick through icing and frosting in continuous motion to make marbleized pattern or heart shapes.

Makes about 2 dozen cupcakes

280

Mini Cocoa Cupcake Kabobs

   1 cup sugar
   1 cup all-purpose flour
⅓ cup HERSHEY'S Cocoa
¾ teaspoon baking powder
¾ teaspoon baking soda
½ teaspoon salt
   1 egg
½ cup milk
¼ cup vegetable oil
   1 teaspoon vanilla extract
½ cup boiling water
   Lickety-Split Cocoa Frosting (recipe follows)
   Jelly beans or sugar nonpareils and/or decorating frosting
   Marshmallows
   Strawberries
   Wooden or metal skewers

282

1. Heat oven to 350°F. Spray small muffin cups (1¾ inches in diameter) with vegetable cooking spray.

2. Stir together sugar, flour, cocoa, baking powder, baking soda and salt in medium bowl. Add egg, milk, oil and vanilla; beat on medium speed of electric mixer 2 minutes. Stir in boiling water (batter will be thin). Fill muffin cups about ⅔ full with batter.

3. Bake 10 minutes or until wooden pick inserted in center comes out clean. Cool slightly; remove from pans to wire racks. Cool completely. Frost with Lickety-Split Cocoa Frosting. Garnish with jelly beans, nonpareils and/or white frosting piped onto cupcake. Alternate cupcakes, marshmallows and strawberries on skewers.   *Makes about 4 dozen cupcakes*

Lickety-Split Cocoa Frosting: Beat 3 tablespoons softened butter or margarine in small bowl until creamy. Add 1¼ cups powdered sugar, ¼ cup HERSHEY'S Cocoa, 2 to 3 tablespoons milk and ½ teaspoon vanilla extract until smooth and of desired consistency. Makes about 1 cup frosting.

Note: Number of kabobs will be determined by length of skewer used and number of cupcakes, marshmallows and strawberries placed on each skewer.

Mini Cocoa Cupcake Kabobs

Surprise Package Cupcakes

  1 package (18 ounces) chocolate cake mix, plus ingredients to prepare mix
  1 container (16 ounces) vanilla frosting
    Food coloring (optional)
  1 tube (4¼ ounces) white decorator icing
72 chewy fruit squares, assorted colors
    Assorted round sprinkles and birthday candles

1. Line standard (2½-inch) muffin cups with paper liners or spray with nonstick cooking spray. Prepare cake mix and bake in muffin cups according to package directions. Cool in pans on wire racks 15 minutes. Remove cupcakes from pans and cool completely.

2. If desired, tint frosting with food coloring, adding a few drops at a time until desired color is reached. Frost cupcakes with white or tinted frosting.

3. Use decorator icing to pipe "ribbons" on fruit squares to resemble wrapped presents. Place 3 candy presents on each cupcake. Decorate with sprinkles and candles as desired.

Makes 24 cupcakes

284

Chocolate Peanut Butter Cups

  1 package DUNCAN HINES® Moist Deluxe® Swiss Chocolate Cake Mix
  1 container DUNCAN HINES® Creamy Home-Style Classic Vanilla Frosting
  ½ cup creamy peanut butter
15 miniature peanut butter cup candies, wrappers removed, cut in half vertically

1. Preheat oven to 350°F. Place 30 (2½-inch) paper liners in muffin cups.

2. Prepare, bake and cool cupcakes following package directions for basic recipe.

3. Combine vanilla frosting and peanut butter in medium bowl. Stir until smooth. Frost one cupcake. Decorate with peanut butter cup candy, cut side down. Repeat with remaining cupcakes, frosting and candies.

Makes 30 servings

Tip: You may substitute Duncan Hines® Moist Deluxe® Devil's Food, Dark Chocolate Fudge or Butter Recipe Fudge Cake Mix flavors for Swiss Chocolate Cake Mix.

Surprise Package Cupcakes

Cookies & Cream Cupcakes

2¼ cups all-purpose flour
1 tablespoon baking powder
½ teaspoon salt
1⅔ cups sugar
1 cup milk
½ cup (1 stick) butter, softened
2 teaspoons vanilla
3 egg whites
1 cup crushed chocolate sandwich cookies (about 10 cookies) plus additional for garnish
1 container (16 ounces) vanilla frosting

1. Preheat oven to 350°F. Line 24 regular-size (2½-inch) muffin pan cups with paper baking cups.

2. Sift flour, baking powder and salt together in large bowl. Stir in sugar. Add milk, butter and vanilla; beat with electric mixer at low speed 30 seconds. Beat at medium speed 2 minutes. Add egg whites; beat 2 minutes. Stir in 1 cup crushed cookies.

3. Spoon batter into prepared muffin cups. Bake 20 to 25 minutes or until toothpick inserted into centers comes out clean. Cool in pans on wire racks 10 minutes. Remove to racks; cool completely.

4. Frost cupcakes; garnish with additional crushed cookies.   *Makes 24 cupcakes*

Snowy Owl Cupcakes

    1 package (about 18 ounces) white cake mix, plus ingredients to prepare mix
    1 container (16 ounces) vanilla frosting
 2½ cups sweetened, shredded coconut
  48 round gummy candies
  24 chocolate-covered coffee beans or black jelly beans
    1 tub (0.6 ounce) black piping gel

Line standard (2½-inch) muffin cups with paper liners or spray with nonstick cooking spray. Prepare cake mix and bake in muffin cups according to package directions. Cool in pans on wire racks 15 minutes. Remove cupcakes from pans and cool completely. Frost cupcakes with vanilla frosting. Sprinkle with coconut to cover completely. Use gummy candies for eyes, coffee beans for beaks and piping gel to dot eyes. *Makes 24 cupcakes*

Triple-Chocolate Cupcakes

    1 package (18.25 ounces) chocolate cake mix
    1 package (4 ounces) chocolate instant pudding and pie filling mix
    1 container (8 ounces) sour cream
    4 large eggs
  ½ cup vegetable oil
  ½ cup warm water
    2 cups (12-ounce package) NESTLÉ® TOLL HOUSE® Semi-Sweet Chocolate Morsels
    2 containers (16 ounces *each*) prepared frosting
       Assorted candy sprinkles

PREHEAT oven to 350°F. Grease or paper-line 30 muffin cups.

COMBINE cake mix, pudding mix, sour cream, eggs, vegetable oil and water in large mixer bowl; beat on low speed just until blended. Beat on high speed for 2 minutes. Stir in morsels. Pour into prepared muffin cups, filling ⅔ full.

BAKE for 25 to 28 minutes or until wooden pick inserted in center comes out clean. Cool in pans for 10 minutes; remove to wire racks to cool completely. Frost; decorate with candy sprinkles. *Makes 30 cupcakes*

Snowy Owl Cupcakes

Peanut Butter Surprise

    2 cups all-purpose flour
    2 teaspoons baking powder
    ¼ teaspoon salt
  1¾ cups sugar
    ½ cup (1 stick) butter, softened
    ¾ cup 2% or whole milk
    1 teaspoon vanilla
    3 large egg whites
    2 (3-ounce) bittersweet chocolate candy bars, melted and cooled
  30 mini peanut butter cups
    1 container prepared chocolate frosting
    3 ounces white chocolate candy bar, broken into chunks

1. Preheat oven to 350°F. Line 30 regular-size (2½-inch) muffin cups with paper baking cups.

2. For cupcakes, combine flour, baking powder and salt in medium bowl; mix well and set aside. Beat sugar and butter with electric mixer at medium speed 1 minute. Add milk and vanilla. Beat with electric mixer at low speed 30 seconds. Gradually beat in flour mixture; beat at medium speed 2 minutes. Add egg whites; beat 1 minute. Stir in melted chocolate.

3. Spoon 1 heaping tablespoon batter into each prepared muffin cup; use back of spoon to slightly spread batter over bottom. Place one mini peanut butter cup in center of each cupcake. Spoon 1 heaping tablespoon batter over peanut butter cup; use back of spoon to smooth out batter. (Do not fill cups more than ¾ full.)

4. Bake 24 to 26 minutes or until puffed and golden brown. Cool in pans on wire racks 10 minutes. (Center of cupcakes will sink slightly upon cooling.) Remove cupcakes to racks; cool completely. (At this point, cupcakes may be frozen up to 3 months.) Spread frosting over cooled cupcakes.

5. For white drizzle, place white chocolate in small resealable plastic food storage bag. Microwave at HIGH (100%) 30 to 40 seconds. Turn bag over; microwave additional 30 seconds or until chocolate is melted. Cut off tiny corner of bag; pipe chocolate decoratively over frosted cupcakes. Store at room temperature up to 24 hours or cover and refrigerate up to 3 days before serving.

Makes 30 cupcakes

290

Berry Surprise Cupcakes

1 package DUNCAN HINES® Moist Deluxe® White Cake Mix
3 egg whites
1⅓ cups water
2 tablespoons vegetable oil
3 sheets (0.5 ounce each) strawberry chewy fruit snacks
1 container DUNCAN HINES® Vanilla Frosting
2 pouches (0.9 ounce each) chewy fruit snack shapes, for garnish (optional)

1. Preheat oven to 350°F. Place 24 (2½-inch) paper liners in muffin cups.

2. Combine cake mix, egg whites, water and oil in large bowl. Beat at low speed with electric mixer until moistened. Beat at medium speed 2 minutes. Fill each liner half full with batter.

3. Cut three fruit snack sheets into 9 equal pieces. (You will have 3 extra squares.) Place each fruit snack piece on top of batter in each cup. Pour remaining batter equally over each. Bake at 350°F for 18 to 23 minutes or until toothpick inserted in center comes out clean. Cool in pans 5 minutes. Remove to cooling racks. Cool completely. Frost cupcakes with Vanilla frosting. Decorate with fruit snack shapes, if desired.   *Makes 12 to 16 servings*

Variation: To make a Berry Surprise Cake, prepare cake following package directions. Pour half the batter into prepared 13×9×2-inch pan. Place 4 fruit snack sheets evenly on top. Pour remaining batter over all. Bake and cool as directed on package. Frost and decorate as described above.

292

His and Hers Cupcakes

1 package (about 18 ounces) cake mix, any flavor, plus ingredients to prepare mix
1 container (16 ounces) vanilla frosting
3 rolls (¾ ounce each) fruit leather
12 pieces striped fruit gum
 Red food coloring
24 vanilla wafer cookies
 Sugar sprinkles

1. Line standard (2½-inch) muffin cups with paper liners or spray with nonstick cooking spray. Prepare cake mix and bake in muffin cups according to package directions. Cool in pans on wire racks 15 minutes. Remove cupcakes from pans and cool completely on wire racks.

2. For "His" cupcakes, frost 12 cupcakes. Cut 4×⅜-inch strips of fruit leather; place 1 strip on each frosted cupcake to form shirt collar. Cut gum into tie shapes; place on cupcakes.

3. For "Hers" cupcakes, tint remaining frosting pink with food coloring. Frost remaining 12 cupcakes with pink frosting. Use small amount of frosting to sandwich two vanilla wafers together; repeat with remaining cookies. Frost cookie "sandwiches" with pink frosting. Top each cupcake with frosted cookie sandwich, placing slightly off-center to form crown of hat. Decorate hats with strips of fruit leather and sprinkles.

Makes 24 cupcakes

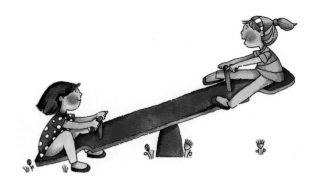

Touchdown Brownie Cups

1 cup (2 sticks) butter or margarine
½ cup HERSHEY¡S Cocoa or HERSHEY¡S Dutch Processed Cocoa
1 cup packed light brown sugar
½ cup granulated sugar
3 eggs
1 teaspoon vanilla extract
1 cup all-purpose flour
1⅓ cup chopped pecans, divided

1. Heat oven to 350°F. Line 2½-inch muffin cups with paper or foil bake cups.

2. Place butter in large microwave-safe bowl; cover. Microwave at HIGH (100%) 1½ minutes or until melted. Add cocoa; stir until smooth. Add brown sugar and granulated sugar; stir until well blended. Add eggs and vanilla; beat well. Add flour and 1 cup pecans; stir until well blended. Fill prepared muffin cups about ¾ full with batter; sprinkle about 1 teaspoon remaining pecans over top of each.

3. Bake 20 to 25 minutes or until tops are beginning to dry and crack. Cool completely in cups on wire rack.
Makes about 17 cupcakes

Touchdown Brownie Cups

Ultimate Rocky Road Cups

¾ cup (1½ sticks) butter or margarine
4 squares (1 ounce each) unsweetened baking chocolate
1½ cups granulated sugar
3 large eggs
1 cup all-purpose flour
1¾ cups "M&M's"® Chocolate Mini Baking Bits
¾ cup coarsely chopped peanuts
1 cup mini marshmallows

Preheat oven to 350°F. Generously grease 24 (2½-inch) muffin cups or line with foil liners. Place butter and chocolate in large microwave-safe bowl. Microwave on HIGH 1 minute; stir. Microwave on HIGH an additional 30 seconds; stir until chocolate is completely melted. Add sugar and eggs, one at a time, beating well after each addition; blend in flour. In separate bowl combine "M&M's"® Chocolate Mini Baking Bits and nuts; stir 1 cup baking bits mixture into brownie batter. Divide batter evenly among prepared muffin cups. Bake 20 minutes. Combine remaining baking bits mixture with marshmallows; divide evenly among muffin cups, topping hot brownies. Return to oven; bake 5 minutes longer. Cool completely before removing from muffin cups. Store in tightly covered container. *Makes 24 cups*

Mini Ultimate Rocky Road Cups: Prepare recipe as directed, dividing batter among 60 generously greased 2-inch mini muffin cups. Bake 15 minutes. Sprinkle with topping mixture; bake 5 minutes longer. Cool completely before removing from cups. Store in tightly covered container. Makes about 60 mini cups.

Ultimate Rocky Road Squares: Prepare recipe as directed, spreading batter into generously greased 13×9×2-inch baking pan. Bake 30 minutes. Sprinkle with topping mixture; bake 5 minutes longer. Cool completely. Cut into squares. Store in tightly covered container. Makes 24 squares.

Chocolate Frosted Peanut Butter Cupcakes

⅓ cup creamy or chunky reduced-fat peanut butter
⅓ cup butter, softened
½ cup granulated sugar
¼ cup packed brown sugar
2 eggs
1 teaspoon vanilla
1¾ cups all-purpose flour
1½ teaspoons baking powder
¼ teaspoon salt
1¼ cups milk
Peanut Butter Chocolate Frosting (recipe follows)

Preheat oven to 350°F. Line 18 (2½-inch) muffin cups with foil baking cups. Beat peanut butter and butter in large bowl with electric mixer at medium speed until smooth; beat in sugars until well mixed. Beat in eggs and vanilla. Combine flour, baking powder and salt; add to peanut butter mixture alternately with milk, beginning and ending with flour mixture. Pour batter into prepared muffin cups. Bake 23 to 25 minutes or until cupcakes spring back when touched and toothpicks inserted in centers come out clean. Cool in pans on wire racks 10 minutes; remove from pans and cool completely. Prepare Peanut Butter Chocolate Frosting. Frost each cupcake with about 1½ tablespoons frosting. *Makes 1½ dozen cupcakes*

Peanut Butter Chocolate Frosting

4 cups powdered sugar
⅓ cup unsweetened cocoa powder
4 to 5 tablespoons milk, divided
3 tablespoons creamy peanut butter

Combine powdered sugar, cocoa, 4 tablespoons milk and peanut butter in large bowl. Beat with electric mixer at low speed until smooth. Beat in additional 1 tablespoon milk until desired spreading consistency. *Makes about 2½ cups frosting*

Chocolate Frosted Peanut Butter Cupcakes

Banana Split Cupcakes

1 package (about 18 ounces) yellow cake mix, divided
1 cup water
1 cup mashed ripe bananas
3 eggs
1 cup chopped drained maraschino cherries
1½ cups miniature semi-sweet chocolate chips, divided
1½ cups prepared vanilla frosting
1 cup marshmallow creme
1 teaspoon shortening
30 whole maraschino cherries, drained and patted dry

1. Preheat oven to 350°F. Line 30 regular-size (2½-inch) muffin cups with paper baking cups.

2. Reserve 2 tablespoons cake mix. Combine remaining cake mix, water, bananas and eggs in large bowl. Beat at low speed of electric mixer until moistened, about 30 seconds. Beat at medium speed 2 minutes. Combine chopped cherries and reserved cake mix in small bowl. Stir chopped cherry mixture and 1 cup chocolate chips into batter.

3. Spoon batter into prepared muffin cups. Bake 15 to 20 minutes or until toothpick inserted into centers comes out clean. Cool in pans on wire racks 10 minutes. Remove to wire racks; cool completely.

4. Combine frosting and marshmallow creme in medium bowl until well blended. Frost each cupcake with frosting mixture.

5. Combine remaining ½ cup chocolate chips and shortening in small microwavable bowl. Microwave at HIGH 30 to 45 seconds, stirring after 30 seconds, or until smooth. Drizzle chocolate mixture over cupcakes. Place one whole cherry on each cupcake.

Makes 30 cupcakes

Note: If desired, omit chocolate drizzle and top cupcakes with colored sprinkles.

302

Color-Bright Ice Cream Sandwiches

¾ cup (1½ sticks) butter or margarine, softened
¾ cup creamy peanut butter
1¼ cups firmly packed light brown sugar
1 large egg
1 teaspoon vanilla extract
1½ cups all-purpose flour
1 teaspoon baking soda
¼ teaspoon salt
1¾ cups "M&M's"® Chocolate Mini Baking Bits, divided
2 quarts vanilla or chocolate ice cream, slightly softened

Preheat oven to 350°F. In large bowl cream butter, peanut butter and sugar until light and fluffy; beat in egg and vanilla. In medium bowl combine flour, baking soda and salt; blend into creamed mixture. Stir in 1⅓ cups "M&M's"® Chocolate Mini Baking Bits. Shape dough into 1¼-inch balls. Place about 2 inches apart on ungreased cookie sheets. Gently flatten to about ½-inch thickness with fingertips. Place 7 or 8 of the remaining "M&M's"® Chocolate Mini Baking Bits on each cookie; press in lightly. Bake 10 to 12 minutes or until edges are light brown. *Do not overbake.* Cool about 1 minute on cookie sheets; cool completely on wire racks. Assemble cookies in pairs with about ⅓ cup ice cream; press cookies together lightly. Wrap each sandwich in plastic wrap; freeze until firm.

Makes about 24 ice cream sandwiches

Creamy Strawberry-Orange Pops

  1 container (8 ounces) strawberry-flavored yogurt
¾ cup orange juice
2 teaspoons vanilla
2 cups frozen whole strawberries
2 teaspoons sugar
6 (7-ounce) paper cups
6 wooden sticks

1. Combine yogurt, orange juice and vanilla in food processor or blender. Process until smooth.

2. Add frozen strawberries and sugar; process until smooth. Pour into 6 paper cups, filling each about ¾ full. Place in freezer for 1 hour. Insert wooden stick into center of each cup. Freeze until solid. Peel off cups before serving. *Makes 6 servings*

Chocolate-Covered Banana Pops

  3 ripe large bananas
9 wooden popsicle sticks
2 cups (12-ounce package) HERSHEY'S Semi-Sweet Chocolate Chips
2 tablespoons shortening (do *not* use butter, margarine, spread or oil)
1½ cups coarsely chopped unsalted, roasted peanuts

1. Peel bananas; cut each into thirds. Insert wooden stick into each banana piece; place on wax paper-covered tray. Cover; freeze until firm.

2. Place chocolate chips and shortening in medium microwave-safe bowl. Microwave at HIGH (100%) 1½ to 2 minutes or until chocolate is melted and mixture is smooth when stirred.

3. Remove bananas from freezer just before dipping. Dip each piece into warm chocolate, covering completely; allow excess to drip off. Immediately roll in peanuts. Cover; return to freezer. Serve frozen. *Makes 9 pops*

Variation: HERSHEY'S Milk Chocolate Chips or HERSHEY'S MINI CHIPS® Semi-Sweet Chocolate Chips may be substituted for Semi-Sweet Chocolate Chips.

Creamy Strawberry-Orange Pops

Peanut Butter Ice Cream Triangles

1½ cups all-purpose flour
½ teaspoon baking powder
½ teaspoon baking soda
¼ teaspoon salt
½ cup butter, softened
½ cup granulated sugar
½ cup packed brown sugar
½ cup creamy peanut butter
1 egg
1 teaspoon vanilla
2½ to 3 cups vanilla, cinnamon or chocolate ice cream, softened

1. Preheat oven to 350°F. Grease cookie sheets.

2. Combine flour, baking powder, baking soda and salt in small bowl; set aside. Beat butter, granulated sugar and brown sugar in large bowl of electric mixer at medium speed until light and fluffy. Beat in peanut butter, egg and vanilla until well blended. Gradually beat in flour mixture on low speed until blended.

3. Divide dough in half. Roll each piece of dough between 2 sheets of waxed paper or plastic wrap into 10×10-inch square, about ⅛ inch thick. Remove top sheet of waxed paper; invert dough onto prepared cookie sheet. Remove second sheet of waxed paper.

4. Score dough into four 4-inch squares. Score each square diagonally into two triangles. *Do not cut completely through dough.* Repeat with remaining dough. Combine excess scraps of dough; roll out and score into additional triangles. Pierce each triangle with fork.

5. Bake 12 to 13 minutes or until set and edges are golden brown. Cool cookies 2 minutes on cookie sheets. Cut through score marks with knife; cool completely on cookie sheets.

6. Place half the cookies on flat surface. Spread ¼ to ⅓ cup softened ice cream on flat side of each cookie; top with remaining cookies. Wrap in plastic wrap and freeze 1 hour or up to 2 days.

Makes about 10 ice cream sandwiches

Peanut Butter Ice Cream Triangle

308

Mice Creams

1 pint vanilla ice cream
1 (4-ounce) package READY CRUST® Mini-Graham Cracker Pie Crusts
  Ears—12 KEEBLER® Grasshopper® cookies
  Tails—3 chocolate twigs, broken in half *or* 6 (3-inch) pieces black shoestring licorice
  Eyes and noses—18 brown candy-coated chocolate candies
  Whiskers—2 teaspoons chocolate sprinkles

1. Place 1 scoop vanilla ice cream into each crust. Press cookie ears and tails into ice cream. Press eyes, noses, and whiskers in place. Serve immediately. Do not refreeze.

Makes 6 servings

Prep Time: 15 minutes

Cherry-Peach Pops

⅓ cup peach nectar or apricot nectar
1 teaspoon unflavored gelatin
1 (15-ounce) can sliced peaches in light syrup, drained
1 (6- or 8-ounce) carton fat-free, sugar-free peach or cherry yogurt
1 (6- or 8-ounce) carton fat-free, sugar-free cherry yogurt

1. Combine nectar and unflavored gelatin in small saucepan; let stand 5 minutes. Heat and stir over low heat just until gelatin dissolves.

2. Combine nectar mixture, drained peaches and yogurts in food processor. Cover and process until smooth.

3. Pour into 7 (3-ounce) paper cups, filling each about ⅔ full. Place in freezer; freeze 1 hour. Insert wooden stick into center of each cup. Freeze at least 3 more hours.

4. Let stand at room temperature 10 minutes before serving. Tear away paper cups to serve.

Makes 7 servings

"M&M's"® Brain Freezer Shake

  2 cups any flavor ice cream
  1 cup milk
  ¾ cup "M&M's"® Chocolate Mini Baking Bits, divided
    Aerosol whipped topping
    Additional "M&M's"® Chocolate Mini Baking Bits for garnish

In blender container combine ice cream and milk; blend until smooth. Add ½ cup "M&M's"® Chocolate Mini Baking Bits; blend just until mixed. Pour into 2 glasses. Top each glass with whipped topping; sprinkle with remaining ¼ cup "M&M's"® Chocolate Mini Baking Bits. Serve immediately. *Makes 2 (1¼-cup) servings*

Kaleidoscope Honey Pops

  2¼ cups water
  ¾ cup honey
  3 cups assorted fruit, cut into small pieces
  12 (3-ounce) paper cups or popsicle molds
  12 popsicle sticks

Whisk together water and honey in pitcher until well blended. Place ¼ cup fruit in each cup. Divide honey mixture between cups. Freeze about 1 hour or until partially frozen. Insert popsicle sticks; freeze until firm and ready to serve. *Makes 12 servings*

*Favorite recipe from **National Honey Board***

Banana Freezer Pops

2 ripe medium bananas
1 can (6 ounces) frozen orange juice concentrate, thawed (¾ cup)
¼ cup water
1 tablespoon honey
1 teaspoon vanilla
8 (3-ounce) paper or plastic cups
8 wooden sticks

1. Peel bananas; break into chunks. Place in food processor or blender container.

2. Add orange juice concentrate, water, honey and vanilla; process until smooth.

3. Pour banana mixture evenly into cups. Cover top of each cup with small piece of aluminum foil. Insert wooden stick through center of foil into banana mixture.

4. Place cups on tray; freeze until firm, about 3 hours. To serve, remove foil; tear off paper cups (or slide out of plastic cups).

Makes 8 servings

314

Peppy Purple Pops: Omit honey and vanilla. Substitute grape juice concentrate for orange juice concentrate.

Frozen Banana Shakes: Increase water to 1½ cups. Prepare fruit mixture as directed. Add 4 ice cubes; process on high speed until mixture is thick and creamy. Makes 3 servings.

Banana Freezer Pops

Chocolate Peanut Butter Ice Cream Sandwiches

2 tablespoons creamy peanut butter
8 chocolate wafer cookies
⅔ cup vanilla ice cream, softened

1. Spread peanut butter over flat sides of all cookies

2. Spoon ice cream over peanut butter on 4 cookies. Top with remaining 4 cookies, peanut butter sides down. Press down lightly to force ice cream to edges of sandwich.

3. Wrap each sandwich in foil; seal tightly. Freeze at least 2 hours or up to 5 days.

Makes 4 servings

Maraschino-Lemonade Pops

316

1 (10-ounce) jar maraschino cherries
1 (12-ounce) can frozen pink lemonade concentrate, partly thawed
¼ cup water
8 (3-ounce) paper cups
8 popsicle sticks

Drain cherries, reserving juice. Place one whole cherry in each paper cup. Coarsely chop remaining cherries. Place chopped cherries, lemonade concentrate, water and reserved juice in container of electric blender or food processor. Purée until smooth. Fill paper cups with equal amounts of cherry mixture. Freeze 30 to 40 minutes or until very slushy. Place popsicle sticks in center of each cup. Freeze 1 hour longer or until firm. To serve, peel off paper cups.

Makes 8 servings

*Favorite recipe from **Cherry Marketing Institute***

Clown-Around Cones

4 waffle cones
½ cup "M&M's"® Chocolate Mini Baking Bits, divided
   Prepared decorator icing
½ cup hot fudge ice cream topping, divided
4 cups any flavor ice cream, softened
1 (1.5- to 2-ounce) chocolate candy bar, chopped
¼ cup caramel ice cream topping

Decorate cones with "M&M's"® Chocolate Mini Baking Bits, using icing to attach; let set. For each cone, place 1 tablespoon fudge topping in bottom of cone. Sprinkle with 1 teaspoon "M&M's"® Chocolate Mini Baking Bits. Layer with ¼ cup ice cream; sprinkle with ¼ of candy bar. Layer with ¼ cup ice cream; sprinkle with 1 teaspoon "M&M's"® Chocolate Mini Baking Bits. Top with 1 tablespoon caramel topping and ½ cup ice cream. Wrap in plastic wrap; freeze until ready to serve. Just before serving, top each cone with 1 tablespoon fudge topping; sprinkle with remaining "M&M's"® Chocolate Mini Baking Bits. *Makes 4 servings*

318

Banana & Chocolate Chip Pops

1 small ripe banana
1 carton (8 ounces) banana yogurt
⅛ teaspoon ground nutmeg
2 tablespoons mini chocolate chips

1. Slice banana; place in food processor with yogurt and nutmeg. Process until smooth. Transfer to small bowl; stir in chips.

2. Spoon banana mixture into 4 plastic popsicle molds. Place tops on molds; set in provided stand. Set on level surface in freezer; freeze 2 hours or until firm. To unmold, briefly run warm water over popsicle molds until each pop loosens. *Makes 4 pops*

Peanut Butter & Jelly Pops: Stir ¼ cup reduced-fat peanut butter in small bowl until smooth; stir in 1 carton (8 ounces) vanilla yogurt. Drop 2 tablespoons all-fruit strawberry preserves on top of mixture; pull spoon back and forth through mixture several times to swirl slightly. Spoon into 4 molds and freeze as directed above. Makes 4 pops.

Blueberry-Lime Pops: Stir 1 carton (8 ounces) Key lime yogurt in small bowl until smooth; fold in ⅓ cup frozen blueberries. Spoon into 4 molds and freeze as directed above. Makes 4 pops.

Clockwise from top: Peanut Butter & Jelly Pop, Blueberry-Lime Pop and Banana & Chocolate Chip Pop

Ice Cream Cookie Sandwich

2 pints chocolate chip ice cream, softened
1 package DUNCAN HINES® Moist Deluxe® Dark Chocolate Fudge Cake Mix
½ cup butter or margarine, softened

1. Line bottom of one 9-inch round cake pan with aluminum foil. Spread ice cream in pan; freeze until firm. Run knife around edge of pan to loosen ice cream. Remove from pan; wrap in foil and return to freezer.

2. Preheat oven to 350°F. Line bottom of two 9-inch round cake pans with aluminum foil. Place cake mix in large bowl. Add butter; mix thoroughly until crumbs form. Place half the cake mix in each prepared pan; press lightly. Bake at 350°F for 15 minutes or until browned around edges; do not overbake. Cool 10 minutes; remove from pans. Remove foil from cookie layers; cool completely.

3. To assemble, place one cookie layer on serving plate. Top with ice cream. Peel off foil. Place second cookie layer on top. Wrap in foil and freeze 2 hours. To keep longer, store in airtight container. Let stand at room temperature for 5 to 10 minutes before cutting.

Makes 10 to 12 servings

Ice Cream Cookie Sandwich

Frozen Berry Ice Cream

8 ounces frozen unsweetened strawberries, partially thawed
8 ounces frozen unsweetened peaches, partially thawed
4 ounces frozen unsweetened blueberries, partially thawed
6 packets sugar substitute
2 teaspoons vanilla
2 cups light vanilla ice cream
16 blueberries
4 small strawberries, halved
8 peach slices

1. Combine frozen strawberries, peaches, blueberries, sugar substitute and vanilla in food processor. Process until coarsely chopped.

2. Add ice cream; process until well blended.

3. Serve immediately for semi-soft texture or freeze until needed and allow to stand 10 minutes to soften slightly. Garnish each serving with 2 blueberries for "eyes," 1 strawberry half for "nose" and 1 peach slice for "smile." *Makes 8 servings (½ cup each)*

Frozen Fudge Pops

½ cup sweetened condensed milk
¼ cup unsweetened cocoa powder
1¼ cups evaporated milk
1 teaspoon vanilla

1. Beat together sweetened condensed milk and cocoa in medium bowl. Add evaporated milk and vanilla; beat until smooth.

2. Pour mixture into 8 small paper cups or 8 popsicle molds. Freeze about 2 hours or until beginning to set. Insert wooden popsicle sticks; freeze until solid. *Makes 8 servings*

Frozen Berry Ice Cream

Brownie Sundae Cake

    1 (19- to 21-ounce) package fudge brownie mix, prepared according to package directions
        for cake-like brownies
    1 cup "M&M's"® Semi-Sweet Chocolate Mini Baking Bits
    ½ cup chopped nuts, optional
    1 quart vanilla ice cream, softened
    ¼ cup caramel or butterscotch ice cream topping

Line 2 (9-inch) round cake pans with aluminum foil, extending slightly over edges of pans. Lightly spray bottoms with vegetable cooking spray; set aside. Preheat oven as brownie mix package directs. Divide brownie batter evenly between pans; sprinkle ½ cup "M&M's"® Semi-Sweet Chocolate Mini Baking Bits and ¼ cup nuts, if desired, over each layer. Bake 23 to 25 minutes or until edges begin to pull away from sides of pans. Cool completely. Remove layers by lifting foil from pans.

To assemble cake, place one brownie layer, topping-side down, in 9-inch springform pan. Carefully spread ice cream over brownie layer; drizzle with ice cream topping. Place second brownie layer on top of ice cream layer, topping-side up; press down lightly. Wrap in plastic wrap and freeze until firm. Remove from freezer about 15 minutes before serving. Remove side of pan. Cut into wedges.

Makes 12 servings

Deep Blue Sea Surprise

    ⅔ cup bottled raspberry/blueberry-flavored juice blend
    ⅓ cup white grape juice
    8 gummy worms or sour night crawlers

1. Combine juices in 2-cup glass measuring cup with pouring spout.

2. Place 2 gummy worms in each of four popsicle molds. Pour ¼ cup juice mixture into each mold. Freeze until solid.

Makes 4 popsicles

Scared Silly

5½ cups cake batter, divided (see note)
1 (15×15-inch) cake board, covered, or large platter
1 container (16 ounces) white frosting
  Food coloring
2 pretzel rods
2 lollipops
2 miniature powdered sugar doughnuts
  Assorted candies and decors

1. Preheat oven to 350°F. Grease and flour 2-quart ovenproof bowl and medium muffin pan. Pour 4 cups cake batter into prepared bowl; pour remaining batter into muffin pan (¼ cup batter per muffin cup). Bake cake in bowl 1 hour and cupcakes about 20 minutes or until wooden skewer inserted into centers comes out clean. Cool 15 minutes in pans. Loosen edges; invert onto wire racks and cool completely.

2. Trim flat side of bowl cake and tops of 2 cupcakes. (Reserve remaining cupcakes for another use.) Place cake on prepared cake board.

3. Tint frosting purple. Frost entire cake and cupcakes with purple frosting.

4. Press pretzel rods into cake about 3 inches apart as shown in photo; press cupcakes into other ends of pretzel rods to create legs and feet of monster. Press lollipops into side of cake to create arms.

5. Position doughnuts on monster for eyes; add assorted candies to create tongue, teeth and toes.

Makes 14 to 18 servings

Note: A traditional cake mix (about 18 ounces) yields about 5½ cups batter per package.

Banana Split Cake

1 package DUNCAN HINES® Moist Deluxe® Banana Supreme Cake Mix
3 eggs
1⅓ cups water
½ cup all-purpose flour
⅓ cup vegetable oil
1 cup mini semisweet chocolate chips
2 to 3 bananas
1 can (16 ounces) chocolate syrup
1 container (8 ounces) frozen whipped topping, thawed
½ cup chopped walnuts
Colored sprinkles
Maraschino cherries with stems, for garnish

1. Preheat oven to 350°F. Grease and flour 13×9×2-inch pan.

2. Combine cake mix, eggs, water, flour and oil in large bowl. Beat at low speed with electric mixer until moistened. Beat at medium speed 2 minutes. Stir in chocolate chips. Pour into prepared pan. Bake at 350°F for 32 to 35 minutes or until toothpick inserted in center comes out clean. Cool completely.

3. Slice bananas. Cut cake into squares; top with banana slices. Drizzle with chocolate syrup. Top with whipped topping, walnuts and sprinkles. Garnish with maraschino cherries.

Makes 12 to 16 servings

Tip: Dip bananas in diluted lemon juice to prevent darkening.

Touchdown!

1 (13×9-inch) cake
1 (19×13-inch) cake board, cut in half crosswise and covered, or large platter
2 cups prepared white frosting
   Food coloring
   Assorted color decorator gels
1 square (2 ounces) almond bark
2 pretzel rods
4 thin pretzel sticks
   Small bear-shaped graham cookies

1. Trim top and sides of cake; place on prepared cake board.

2. Tint frosting medium green.

3. Frost entire cake with green frosting. Pipe field lines with white decorator gel.

4. Melt almond bark in tall glass according to package directions. Break off one quarter of each pretzel rod; discard shorter pieces. Break 2 pretzel sticks in half. Dip pretzels in melted almond bark, turning to coat completely and tapping off excess. Using pretzel rods for support posts, pretzel sticks for crossbars and pretzel stick halves for uprights, arrange pretzels in two goalpost formations on waxed paper; let stand until completely dry. When dry, carefully peel waxed paper from goalposts; place on each end of cake.

5. Meanwhile, decorate bear-shaped cookies with decorator gels; position cookies throughout field as desired.

Makes 16 to 20 servings

Fudge Ribbon Cake

1 (18.25-ounce) package chocolate cake mix
1 (8-ounce) package cream cheese, softened
2 tablespoons butter or margarine, softened
1 tablespoon cornstarch
1 (14-ounce) can EAGLE BRAND® Sweetened Condensed Milk (NOT evaporated milk)
1 egg
1 teaspoon vanilla extract
    Chocolate Glaze (recipe follows)

1. Preheat oven to 350°F. Grease and flour 13×9-inch baking pan. Prepare cake mix as package directs. Pour batter into prepared pan.

2. In small mixing bowl, beat cream cheese, butter and cornstarch until fluffy. Gradually beat in Eagle Brand. Add egg and vanilla; beat until smooth. Spoon evenly over cake batter.

3. Bake 40 minutes or until wooden pick inserted near center comes out clean. Cool. Prepare Chocolate Glaze and drizzle over cake. Store covered in refrigerator.

Makes 10 to 12 servings

334

Chocolate Glaze: In small saucepan over low heat, melt 1 (1-ounce) square unsweetened or semi-sweet chocolate and 1 tablespoon butter or margarine with 2 tablespoons water. Remove from heat. Stir in ¾ cup powdered sugar and ½ teaspoon vanilla extract. Stir until smooth and well blended. Makes about ⅓ cup.

Fudge Ribbon Bundt Cake: Preheat oven to 350°F. Grease and flour 10-inch Bundt pan. Prepare cake mix as package directs. Pour batter into prepared pan. Prepare cream cheese layer as directed above; spoon evenly over batter. Bake 50 to 55 minutes or until wooden pick inserted near center comes out clean. Cool 10 minutes. Remove from pan. Cool. Prepare Chocolate Glaze and drizzle over cake. Store covered in refrigerator.

Prep Time: 20 minutes
Bake Time: 40 minutes

Fudge Ribbon Cake

Campfire Fun

2 (9-inch) square chocolate cake layers
1 (10-inch) square cake board, covered, or large plate
1 cup chocolate chips
½ cup heavy cream
2¼ cups prepared white frosting, divided
¾ cup marshmallow creme
1 tablespoon unsweetened cocoa powder
¼ cup graham cracker crumbs
¼ cup peanut butter chips

1. Trim tops and sides of cake layers. Place one layer on prepared cake board.

2. For chocolate filling, heat chocolate chips and cream in microwavable bowl at HIGH (100%) 1 minute or until chocolate is melted; stir until smooth. Chill 10 minutes, stirring occasionally, or until filling reaches desired consistency. (Filling will thicken as it cools.)

3. For marshmallow filling, combine ¾ cup frosting and marshmallow creme in small bowl; stir until smooth.

4. Combine remaining 1½ cups frosting and cocoa; stir until smooth. Frost sides of bottom cake layer with cocoa frosting; let stand 10 minutes to set frosting.

5. Spread chocolate filling over cake layer, allowing some filling to run over edges. Spread marshmallow filling over chocolate filling, allowing some filling to run over edges. Place second cake layer over marshmallow filling.

6. Frost top and sides of top cake layer with cocoa frosting. Sprinkle graham cracker crumbs over top of cake; press in lightly. Arrrange peanut butter chips over top of cake. Score cake down center to resemble graham cracker perforations as shown in photo.

Makes 16 to 18 servings

Note: When preparing the cake, either from scratch or a mix, use ¾ of the batter in a 9-inch square pan to make a higher cake. Bake remaining batter in paper-lined muffin pan cups or reserve for another use.

336

Carousel Cake

1 (10-inch) bundt cake
1 (10-inch) round cake board, covered, or large plate
1 container (16 ounces) white frosting
   Food coloring
   Assorted animal-shaped cookies
   Decorator gel (optional)
   Assorted candies and decors
   Colored or striped drinking straws
   Paper carousel roof (see tip)

1. Place cake on prepared cake board.

2. Tint frosting orange. Frost cake with orange frosting, allowing frosting to drip down side of cake.

3. Outline animal-shaped cookies with decorator gel, if desired; arrange cookies on top of cake. Press candies and decors lightly into frosting.

4. Place straws around cake to support carousel roof; carefully set roof on top of straws.

Makes 14 to 16 servings

Tip: To create the carousel roof, cut out a 7½-inch circle from an 8½×11-inch sheet of construction paper. Cut one slit from the outer edge of the circle to the center; tape the cut edges together to form the carousel roof. If a two-color carousel roof is desired, cut a second 7½-inch circle from construction paper in another color and fold it into 8 wedges. Carefully cut out 4 wedges; glue them onto the first circle of paper so the colors alternate (before cutting the slit and taping the edges).

Buzzz

4 cups cake batter (see note)
1 (10-inch) round cake board, covered, or large plate
1¾ cups prepared white frosting
    Food coloring
    Assorted black, yellow and red candies
    Black licorice twists

1. Preheat oven to 350°F. Grease and flour 2½-quart ovenproof bowl. Pour cake batter into prepared bowl. Bake 60 to 70 minutes or until wooden skewer inserted into center comes out clean. Cool 15 minutes in bowl. Loosen edge; invert onto wire rack and cool completely.

2. Trim flat side of cake. Turn cake over and cut small piece from top of cake to slightly flatten back of bee, if desired. Place cake on prepared cake board.

3. Reserve ¼ cup white frosting. Tint ¾ cup frosting black and ¾ cup frosting yellow.

4. Using wooden toothpick, mark semicircle about 3½ inches from one edge of cake for face, and 3 parallel semicircles for rest of body.

5. Frost face with reserved white frosting. Alternately frost body sections with yellow and black, piping frosting with floral tip to create fuzzy texture, if desired. Reserve small portion of black frosting for piping.

6. Using medium writing tip and reserved black frosting, pipe line between head and body. Arrange assorted candies and licorice twists for face, antennae, legs, wings and stinger as shown in photo.

Makes 14 to 18 servings

Note: A traditional cake mix (about 18 ounces) yields about 5½ cups batter per package.

Kids' Confetti Cake

CAKE
- 1 package DUNCAN HINES® Moist Deluxe® Classic Yellow Cake Mix
- 1 package (4-serving size) vanilla-flavor instant pudding and pie filling mix
- 4 eggs
- 1 cup water
- ½ cup vegetable oil
- 1 cup mini semisweet chocolate chips

TOPPING
- 1 cup colored miniature marshmallows
- ⅔ cup DUNCAN HINES® Creamy Home-Style Chocolate Frosting
- 2 tablespoons mini semisweet chocolate chips

1. Preheat oven to 350°F. Grease and flour 13×9×2-inch baking pan.

2. For cake, combine cake mix, pudding mix, eggs, water and oil in large bowl. Beat at medium speed with electric mixer 2 minutes. Stir in 1 cup chocolate chips. Pour into prepared pan. Bake at 350°F for 40 to 45 minutes or until toothpick inserted in center comes out clean.

3. For topping, immediately arrange marshmallows evenly over hot cake. Place frosting in microwave-safe bowl. Microwave at HIGH (100% power) 25 to 30 seconds. Stir until smooth. Drizzle evenly over marshmallows and cake. Sprinkle with 2 tablespoons chocolate chips. Cool completely. *Makes 12 to 16 servings*

Kids' Confetti Cake

342

Out of This World

4½ cups cake batter, divided (see note)
1 (10-inch) round cake board, covered, or large plate
1¾ cups prepared white frosting
    Food coloring
    Red decorator gel
    Black licorice twists
8 to 10 large gumballs
    Assorted candies

1. Preheat oven to 350°F. Grease and flour 9-inch round cake pan and 1½-quart ovenproof bowl. Pour 2¾ cups cake batter into prepared cake pan; pour 1¾ cups cake batter into prepared bowl. Bake cake in pan 30 to 35 minutes and cake in bowl 45 to 55 minutes or until wooden skewer inserted into centers comes out clean. Cool 15 minutes in pans. Loosen edges; invert onto wire racks and cool completely.

2. Trim top of bowl cake and top and side of round cake. Place round cake on prepared cake board. Spread small amount of frosting on center of round cake. Place bowl cake, flat side down, on top of round cake.

3. Reserve ¼ cup frosting; tint remaining 1½ cups frosting blue-gray.

4. Frost entire cake with blue-gray frosting. Frost top half of round cake with white frosting (over blue-gray frosting). Cover top of round cake with red decorator gel.

5. Cut licorice twists into 1½-inch pieces; arrange on side of bowl cake as shown in photo. Decorate UFO with gumballs and assorted candies as shown in photo.

Makes 12 to 14 servings

Note: A traditional cake mix (about 18 ounces) yields about 5½ cups batter per package.

Slinky the Snake

2 (10-inch) bundt cakes
1 (40×20-inch) cake board, covered
2 containers (16 ounces each) white frosting
 Food coloring
1 cup semisweet chocolate chips
 Red fruit rollup
 Assorted candies

1. Cut each bundt cake in half. Position each half end to end to form one long serpentine shape as shown in photo. Place on prepared cake board, attaching pieces with small amount of frosting.

2. Tint frosting lime green. Frost entire length of cake with green frosting, spreading frosting about halfway down sides of cake.

3. Place chocolate chips in small plastic food storage bag. Microwave on MEDIUM (50% power) 20 seconds. Knead bag several times, then microwave 20 seconds more until chocolate is melted. Cut tip off one corner of bag; pipe diamond pattern for scales on back of snake as shown in photo.

4. Cut out tongue and other decorations from fruit rollups. Decorate face and back of snake with assorted candies.

Makes 32 to 36 servings

346

Flapjack Party Stack

1 package (about 18 ounces) yellow cake mix, plus ingredients to prepare mix
1 container (16 ounces) vanilla frosting
1 quart fresh strawberries, washed, hulled and sliced
1 cup caramel or butterscotch ice cream topping

1. Preheat oven to 350°F. Grease bottom and sides of 4 (9-inch) round cake pans with nonstick cooking spray; line bottoms with waxed paper. Prepare and bake cake mix according to package directions (reduce baking time for thinner cake layers). Remove from oven and let cool in pans 15 minutes. Remove from pans and cool completely on wire racks.

2. Place 1 cake layer on serving plate; frost top only with frosting swirls resembling whipped butter. Top with layer of sliced strawberries. Repeat with next 2 cake layers. Top stack with remaining cake layer. Pile frosting in center of stack; top with remaining strawberries.

3. Heat caramel topping in microwave just until pourable. Drizzle generous amount of topping over cake stack to resemble syrup on stack of pancakes.   *Makes 12 servings*

348

Quick Rocky Road Cake

1 package DUNCAN HINES® Moist Deluxe® Devil's Food Cake Mix
1 container DUNCAN HINES® Creamy Home-Style Classic Vanilla Frosting
½ cup creamy peanut butter
⅓ cup semi-sweet chocolate chips
⅓ cup salted cocktail peanuts

1. Preheat oven to 350°F. Grease and flour 13×9×2-inch pan.

2. Prepare, bake and cool cake following package directions for basic recipe.

3. Combine Vanilla Frosting and peanut butter in medium bowl. Frost top of cake. Sprinkle with chocolate chips and peanuts.   *Makes 12 to 16 servings*

Tip: For an easy treat for kids, follow package directions for making cupcakes. Frost and decorate as directed above.

Party Time

5½ cups cake batter, divided (see note)
1 (14-inch round) cake board, covered, or large plate
1½ cups prepared white frosting
    Food coloring
    Black and green decorator gels
    Black licorice twists
    Red licorice rope
    Assorted candies
2 gum-filled lollipops

1. Preheat oven to 350°F. Grease and flour 9-inch round cake pan and medium muffin pan. Pour 3½ cups cake batter into cake pan; pour remaining cake batter into muffin pan (¼ cup batter per muffin cup). Bake cake in pan 35 to 45 minutes and cupcakes about 20 minutes or until toothpick inserted into centers comes out clean. Cool 15 minutes in pans. Loosen edges; invert onto wire racks and cool completely.

2. Trim top and side of round cake and two cupcakes. (Reserve remaining cupcakes for another use.) Place round cake on prepared cake board.

3. Tint half of frosting purple.

4. Frost top of round cake with white frosting. Frost side of cake and cupcakes with purple frosting. Position cupcakes with tops against side of round cake as shown in photo; attach cupcakes to round cake with small amount of purple frosting. Pipe decorative edge around face of clock and edges of cupcakes, if desired.

5. Pipe numbers and dots on face of clock with decorator gels. Arrange licorice and candies for clock hands and stopper as shown in photo.

6. Insert lollipops into bottom of clock for feet.

Makes 12 to 14 servings

Note: A traditional cake mix (about 18 ounces) yields about 5½ cups batter per package.

Nessie

2 (10-inch) bundt cakes
2½ cups prepared white frosting
Food coloring
1 (40×20-inch) cake board, covered
Gumballs, assorted candies and red licorice twist

1. Cut one bundt cake in half. Cut second Bundt cake in quarters; set aside two quarters for another use.

2. Tint frosting light purple.

3. Frost two bundt cake halves with frosting, covering all sides of cake except two cut surfaces on each half. Frost two bundt cake quarters with frosting, covering all sides of cake except one cut surface on each quarter.

4. Stand two bundt cake halves on their cut surfaces, positioning them end to end in center of prepared cake board. Place bundt cake quarters, unfrosted cut surfaces down, on either side of bundt cake halves to resemble Loch Ness monster's head and tail as shown in photo.

5. Decorate monster with gumballs, assorted candies and licorice as shown in photo.

Makes 24 to 28 servings

Pretty Package Cake

1 package (about 18 ounces) lemon cake mix, plus ingredients to prepare mix
1 container (16 ounces) lemon frosting

RIBBON DOUGH
1 cup marshmallow cream
2 cups powdered sugar, sifted
Red food coloring

COOKIE GARNISH (OPTIONAL)
1 package (18 ounces) refrigerated sugar cookie dough
1 tube (4¼ ounces) pink decorator icing
1 tube (4¼ ounces) yellow decorator icing
1 tube (4¼ ounces) green decorator icing

1. Prepare and bake cake in two 8-inch square baking pans according to package directions. Cool completely and remove from pans. Place one cake layer on serving plate; top with lemon frosting and second cake layer. Frost top and sides of cake.

2. For Ribbon Dough, mix marshmallow creme and powdered sugar in medium bowl; stir until blended. Knead by hand until dough is stiff and workable. (Sprinkle sifted powdered sugar on hands often to keep dough from sticking.) Knead in 2 to 3 drops of food coloring until desired ribbon color is reached. Roll out dough ¼ inch thick on cutting board, sprinkling with sifted powdered sugar as necessary to prevent sticking. Cut into strips about 1½ inches wide.

3. Lay strips over frosted cake to form ribbon and bow; trim ends. If desired, prepare 2-inch round cookies from cookie dough; bake according to package directions. Let cool on wire rack. Pipe flowers on cookies with decorator icing in assorted colors. Garnish cake with cookies.

Makes 12 to 16 servings

Tip: This great all-occasion cake can be easily customized for any celebration. Simply frost with appropriate colors and decorate the cookies to match the theme.

Picasso's Palette

   1 (9-inch) round cake
   1 (10-inch) round cake board, covered, or large plate
   1 cup prepared white frosting
     Food coloring
     Assorted color decorator gels
     Red pull-apart licorice twist
   1 pretzel rod

1. Trim top and side of cake. Cut out small circle on one side of cake; cut piece from side of cake to create palette shape as shown in photo. Place on prepared cake board.

2. Tint frosting light brown.

3. Frost entire cake with brown frosting. Pipe spots of paint on palette with decorator gels.

4. Create artist's paintbrush by cutting 2-inch lengths of licorice and attaching them to pretzel rod with foil as shown in photo. *Makes 10 to 12 servings*

356

Banana Fudge Layer Cake

   1 package DUNCAN HINES® Moist Deluxe® Yellow Cake Mix
1⅓ cups water
   3 eggs
⅓ cup vegetable oil
   1 cup mashed ripe bananas (about 3 medium)
   1 container DUNCAN HINES® Chocolate Frosting

1. Preheat oven to 350°F. Grease and flour two 9-inch round cake pans.

2. Combine cake mix, water, eggs and oil in large bowl. Beat at low speed with electric mixer until moistened. Beat at medium speed 2 minutes. Stir in bananas.

3. Pour into prepared pans. Bake at 350°F for 28 to 31 minutes or until toothpick inserted in center comes out clean. Cool in pans 15 minutes. Remove from pans; cool completely.

4. Fill and frost cake with frosting. Garnish as desired. *Makes 12 to 16 servings*

It's My Party

5½ cups cake batter, divided (see note)
1 (10-inch) round prepared cake board, covered, or large plate
2 container (16 ounces each) white frosting
Food coloring
1 doll
Assorted candies and decors

1. Preheat oven to 350°F. Grease and flour 2-quart ovenproof bowl and 8-inch round cake pan. Pour 3½ cups cake batter into prepared bowl; pour 2 cups cake batter into cake pan. Bake cake in bowl 55 to 60 minutes and cake in pan 25 to 30 minutes or until wooden skewer inserted into centers comes out clean. Cool 15 minutes in pans. Loosen edges; invert on wire racks and cool completely.

2. Trim flat side of bowl cake and top of round cake. Trim side of round cake so edge is even with bowl cake. Place round cake on prepared cake board.

3. Frost top of round cake lightly with frosting. Place bowl cake, flat side down, on top of round cake.

4. Tint 1 cup frosting purple.

5. Frost entire cake with white frosting.

6. Make small cut in center of cake and insert doll into cake. (To keep doll's clothing clean, wrap bottom of doll in plastic wrap.)

7. Using medium writing tip and purple frosting, pipe designs on party dress. Decorate with assorted candies and decors as shown in photo. *Makes 14 to 18 servings*

Note: A traditional cake mix (about 18 ounces) yields about 5½ cups batter per package.

Fudgy Ripple Cake

> 1 package (18.25 ounces) yellow cake mix plus ingredients to prepare mix
> 1 package (3 ounces) cream cheese, softened
> 2 tablespoons unsweetened cocoa powder
>   Fudgy Glaze (recipe follows)
> ½ cup "M&M's"® Chocolate Mini Baking Bits

Preheat oven to 350°F. Lightly grease and flour 10-inch Bundt or ring pan; set aside. Prepare cake mix as package directs. In medium bowl combine 1½ cups prepared batter, cream cheese and cocoa powder until smooth. Pour half of yellow batter into prepared pan. Drop spoonfuls of chocolate batter over yellow batter in pan. Top with remaining yellow batter. Bake about 45 minutes or until toothpick inserted near center comes out clean. Cool completely on wire rack. Unmold cake onto serving plate. Prepare Fudgy Glaze; spread over top of cake, allowing some glaze to run over side. Sprinkle with "M&M's"® Chocolate Mini Baking Bits. Store in tightly covered container.

Makes 10 servings

360

Fudgy Glaze

> 1 square (1 ounce) semi-sweet chocolate
> 1 cup powdered sugar
> ⅓ cup unsweetened cocoa powder
> 3 tablespoons milk
> ½ teaspoon vanilla extract

Place chocolate in small microwave-safe bowl. Microwave at HIGH 30 seconds; stir. Repeat as necessary until chocolate is completely melted, stirring at 10-second intervals; set aside. In medium bowl combine powdered sugar and cocoa powder. Stir in milk, vanilla and melted chocolate until smooth.

Stripes

5½ cups cake batter, divided (see note)
1 (10-inch) round cake board, covered, or large platter
1 container (16 ounces) white frosting
Food coloring
3 chocolate sandwich cookies
1 individual chocolate-covered cake roll
Pretzel sticks
Chocolate sprinkles
Assorted candies and red licorice whip

1. Preheat oven to 350°F. Grease and flour 9-inch round cake pan and medium muffin pan. Pour 3½ cups cake batter into cake pan; pour remaining cake batter into muffin pan (¼ cup batter per muffin cup). Bake cake in pan 35 to 45 minutes and cupcakes about 20 minutes or until toothpick inserted into centers comes out clean. Cool 15 minutes in pans. Loosen edges; invert onto wire racks and cool completely.

2. Trim tops and sides of round cake and two cupcakes. (Reserve remaining cupcakes for another use.) Place cake on prepared cake board. Position two cupcakes next to cake to form ears.

3. Tint frosting orange.

4. Frost entire cake and cupcakes with orange frosting.

5. Carefully open two sandwich cookies to expose white filling. Place opened cookies on tiger's ears. Cut two thin slices from cake roll; place on tiger's face for eyes.

6. Add pretzel whiskers, cookie nose, candy mouth and chocolate sprinkle stripes as shown in photo.

Makes 12 to 14 servings

Note: A traditional cake mix (about 18 ounces) yields about 5½ cups batter per package.

Crayon Craze

1 (13×9-inch) cake
1 (14×10-inch) cake board, covered, or large platter
2 containers (16 ounces each) white frosting
   Food coloring
4 flat-bottomed ice cream cones

1. Trim top and sides of cake. Measure 4½ inches down long sides of cake; draw line across top of cake with wooden toothpick to create 9×4½-inch rectangle. Using toothpick line as guide, carefully cut halfway through cake (about 1 inch). Do *not* cut all the way through cake.

2. Cut cake in half horizontally from 9-inch side just to horizontal cut made at 4½-inch line. Remove 9×4½×1-inch piece of cake; reserve for another use. Round edges of 9-inch side to resemble top of crayon box as shown in photo. Place cake on prepared cake board.

3. Tint 1 container frosting gold. Tint 1 cup frosting green. Divide remaining frosting into 4 parts (about ¼ cup each). Tint one part red, one yellow, one orange and one blue.

4. Frost entire cake with gold frosting. Using medium writing tip and green frosting, pipe the word CRAYONS on cake. Pipe stripes and two green triangles on bottom of box and decorative borders around box as shown in photo.

5. Gently cut ice cream cones in half vertically with serrated knife. Frost each of four cone halves different color (red, yellow, orange and blue). Place frosted cones on cake, just below rounded edge, to resemble crayon tips.

Makes 16 to 18 servings

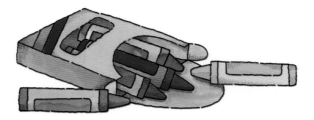

Cookies 'n' Cream Cake

1 package (about 18 ounces) white cake mix
1 package (4-serving size) instant white chocolate-flavored pudding and pie filling mix
1 cup vegetable oil
4 egg whites
½ cup milk
20 chocolate sandwich cookies, coarsely chopped
½ cup semisweet chocolate chips
1 teaspoon vegetable shortening
4 chocolate sandwich cookies, cut into quarters for garnish

1. Preheat oven to 350°F. Spray 10-inch fluted tube pan with nonstick cooking spray.

2. Beat cake mix, pudding mix, oil, egg whites and milk 2 minutes in large bowl with electric mixer at medium speed or until ingredients are well blended. Stir in chopped cookies; spread in prepared pan.

3. Bake 50 to 60 minutes or until cake springs back when lightly touched. Cool 1 hour in pan on wire rack. Invert cake onto serving plate; cool completely.

4. Combine chocolate chips and shortening in glass measuring cup. Heat in microwave at HIGH (100%) power 1 minute; stir. Continue heating at 15 second intervals, stirring until melted and smooth. Drizzle glaze over cake and garnish with quartered cookies.

Makes 10 to 12 servings

Turtle Cake

    1 package DUNCAN HINES® Moist Deluxe® Fudge Marble Cake Mix
    6 fun-size chocolate-covered nougat, caramel, peanut candy bars
    1 container (16 ounces) DUNCAN HINES® Creamy Home-Style Cream Cheese Frosting,
       divided
      Green food coloring
    2 tablespoons slivered almonds
      Candy-coated chocolate pieces
      White chocolate chips

1. Preheat oven to 350°F. Grease and flour 2½-quart ovenproof glass bowl with rounded bottom.

2. Prepare cake following package directions for original recipe. Pour into prepared bowl. Bake at 350°F for 55 to 60 minutes or until toothpick inserted in center comes out clean. Cool in bowl 20 minutes. Invert onto cooling rack. Cool completely.

3. Place cake on serving plate. Remove 1-inch cake square from upper side of cake for head. Insert 2 fun-size candy bars, flat sides together, into square hole for head. Position remaining 4 candy bars under cake for feet. Reserve 1 teaspoon Cream Cheese frosting. Tint remaining Cream Cheese frosting with green food coloring; frost cake. Sprinkle almonds on top. Place candy-coated chocolate pieces around bottom edge of shell. Attach white chocolate chips to head with reserved frosting for eyes.

Makes 12 to 16 servings

368

Ballet Slippers

1 package (about 18 ounces) white cake mix with pudding, plus ingredients to
   prepare mix
1 container (16 ounces) vanilla frosting, divided
   Red food coloring
1 tube (4¼ ounces) pink decorator icing
   Pink ribbon

1. Prepare cake mix and bake in 13×9-inch baking pan according to package directions. Cool completely; remove from pan and place on cookie sheet in freezer several hours or overnight.

2. Cut frozen cake in half lengthwise, then cut each half into ballet slipper shape as shown in photo. Arrange slippers on serving platter. Place remaining cake pieces in plastic bag and freeze for another use.

3. Remove ⅓ cup frosting and reserve. Tint remaining frosting with red food coloring to desired shade of pink. Frost center of each shoe with reserved white frosting, leaving 1 inch on each side and 3 inches at toe and heel. Frost rest of slippers with pink frosting as shown in photo. To add texture, lightly press cheesecloth into frosting and lift off. Outline soles and centers of shoes with pink decorator icing.

4. Tie ribbon into two bows; place on toes of ballet shoes before serving.

Makes 12 to 16 servings

Around the World

5½ cups cake batter, divided (see note)
1 (15×15-inch) cake board, covered
1 container (16 ounces) white frosting
   Food coloring
1 pretzel rod, broken in half
3 chocolate licorice twists
   Green gumdrops

1. Preheat oven to 350°F. Grease and flour 9-inch cake pan, 6-ounce custard cup and medium muffin pan. Pour 3½ cups cake batter into cake pan, ½ cup cake batter into custard cup and remaining batter into muffin pan (¼ cup battter per muffin cup). Bake cake in pan 35 to 45 minutes, cake in custard cup about 25 minutes and cupcakes about 20 minutes or until toothpick inserted into centers comes out clean. Cool 15 minutes in pans. Loosen edges; invert onto wire racks and cool completely.

2. Trim top and side of round cake. Cut custard cup cake vertically in half. Arrange round cake, one cupcake (upside down) and half of custard cup cake on prepared cake board as shown in photo. (Reserve remaining cupcakes for another use.)

3. Reserve ½ cup frosting. Tint remaining frosting blue. Divide reserved frosting in half; tint ¼ cup frosting orange and ¼ cup green.

4. Frost entire round cake with blue frosting. Frost cupcake with green frosting and custard cup half with orange frosting.

5. Position pretzel rod halves to look as though they are running through globe at North and South Poles. Arrange licorice twists to connect pretzel rods to base of globe as shown in photo.

6. Flatten gumdrops with rolling pin on smooth, flat surface or sheet of waxed paper sprinkled with sugar. Roll until very thin (about ⅟₁₆ inch), turning frequently to coat with sugar. Cut gumdrops into shapes of continents with sharp knife or scissors. Arrange continents on globe as shown in photo.   *Makes 12 to 14 servings*

Note: A traditional cake mix (about 18 ounces) yields about 5½ cups batter per package.

372

ACKNOWLEDGMENTS

The publisher would like to thank the companies and organizations listed below for the use of their recipes and photographs in this publication.

Bestfoods

Birds Eye®

Bob Evans®

Cherry Marketing Institute

ConAgra Grocery Products Company

Del Monte Corporation

Dole Food Company, Inc.

Domino Sugar Corporation

Duncan Hines® and Moist Deluxe® are registered trademarks of Aurora Foods Inc.

Eagle® Brand

Egg Beaters®

The Golden Grain Company®

Grandma's® is a registered trademark of Mott's, Inc.

Hebrew National®

Hershey Foods Corporation

Hillshire Farm®

The HV Company

Lawry's® Foods, Inc.

©Mars, Inc. 2002

Mott's® is a registered trademark of Mott's, Inc.

Nabisco Biscuit Company

National Honey Board

Nestlé USA, Inc.

New York Apple Association, Inc.

Ortega®

Peanut Advisory Board

Perdue Farms Incorporated

The Procter & Gamble Company

The Quaker® Oatmeal Kitchens

Reckitt Benckiser

Sargento® Foods Inc.

The J.M. Smucker Company

StarKist® Seafood Company

The Sugar Association, Inc.

Reprinted with permission of Sunkist Growers, Inc.

Texas Peanut Producers Board

Tyson Foods, Inc.

Unilever Bestfoods North America

Wisconsin Milk Marketing Board

374

INDEX